LIFE
INSIDE
OUT

How I Found True Freedom in God

Mark Foss

LIFE SENTENCE
Publishing, LLC

Visit the LifeRight website: www.liferightoutreach.org:

Life Inside Out – Mark Foss

Copyright © 2015

First edition published 2015

Cover Design: Amber Burger

Cover Photography: BortN66/Shutterstock

Editors: Donna Sundblad, Ruth Zetek

Printed in the United States of America

By Aneko Press – *Our Readers Matter*™

www.anekopress.com

Aneko Press, Life Sentence Publishing, and our logos are trademarks of Life Sentence Publishing, Inc.

203 E. Birch Street
P.O. Box 652
Abbotsford, WI 54405

BIOGRAPHY & AUTOBIOGRAPHY / Religious

Paperback ISBN: 978-1-62245-257-6

Ebook ISBN: 978-1-62245-258-3

10   9   8   7   6   5   4   3   2   1

Available wherever books are sold.

Share this book on Facebook:

Contents

I dedicate this book to my father and mother, Harold (Harry) and Isabell Foss, who I love and respect with all my heart.

CHAPTER 1

Walking Away from Innocence

We all, like sheep, have gone astray, each of us has turned to our own way; and the Lord has laid on him the iniquity of us all. (Isaiah 53:6)

I would call growing up in a small town in west-central Minnesota a blessing. Hancock was a small town. When I say small, I'm talking about a population of about nine hundred people. Born in 1957, I reached my teenage years in 1970, a turbulent time in America. The Vietnam War was raging and people were protesting. The theme of the day was "drugs, sex, and rock-n-roll."

While Hancock was primarily a farming town, the actual town itself consisted of two grocery stores, several gas stations, two hardware stores, three restaurants, a drug store, a bakery, a bank, and a couple of bars. Today almost all of these are gone except for a bar and a gas station.

The main employer in town was a business called Hancock Concrete. It's been in the Schmidgall family for decades and builds culverts, drain pipes, and arch pipes for road construction. A lot of people in Hancock and the surrounding towns have made a career out of working there.

My mom and dad came from two totally different family types. Dad had one sister, Vera Jensen, and very few relatives. My mother came from a family of six brothers and six sisters; age-wise, she was right in the middle. I grew up not knowing either of my grandpas. My Grandpa Peter Swanberg died in 1964, when I was four years old. Dad's dad died when he was about fourteen. A while later his mother remarried a man whom my dad did not get along with. After graduating from high school, my dad joined the navy and the Merchant Marines. While in the service, he worked in the mailroom, which became his career when he got out. He eventually retired at age fifty-five with about thirty years of service to the government.

As a young boy, I really enjoyed making people laugh, whether it was by acting like a monkey or being quick with a comment. I tended to get into mischief and lived the life of a typical class clown. This trait became a nightmare for most of my teachers throughout my school years, but to me it was all good-natured fun. But I changed. Instead of being the boy who made people laugh, I turned into a person who brought unhappiness. My life took a path my parents didn't see coming. For that matter, I didn't see it coming either.

I didn't set out to hurt the people who loved me. I just eased into a life of doing what I liked, and by the time I was thirteen, that included weed and alcohol. Along with my newfound pastimes, my otherwise petty mischief turned into stealing, vandalism, etc. My ability to get along with others changed too. In fact, it wasn't out of the ordinary to see me in a fight or being a smart aleck to the older guys.

Before that happened, I lived in a "normal" family as the fourth of five kids. My brother, Brad, was the oldest – six years older than me. My sister Lynn was five years older, Annette was three years older, and my little sister, Lori, was five years younger.

Back in the '60s, before my life got off track, I lived a typical small-town life in Minnesota. We roamed the town without worry and rode our bikes everywhere. I played over at friends' houses until I was called home for dinner. The distance to any-one's house was, at the most, probably a mile. We played a lot of baseball, football, and basketball. Back then, I also had an interest in and a talent for singing. I sang in the church choir and also in school. It wasn't unusual for me to sing solos. I even had a lead part in an operetta in the sixth grade as a big, white bunny that grew bright red wings. (It's crazy, but the only words I remember from that play were from a song I sang that said, "Oh, how I wish, oh, how I wish that I could be somebody else.") Don't think I didn't pay for that wish for about twenty years. I probably shouldn't even mention it now, as it will undoubtedly bring it back to the forefront of the minds of a few who have long forgotten.

A typical day started with my siblings and me getting up and having cocoa and toast (our favorite) before heading off to school. As a grade-schooler, I walked to school about four blocks away. My dog, Princess, a Springer Spaniel, watched me go and faithfully waited for me to come home. Once in a while, one of my Brother Brad's friends would pick me up and give me a ride in his souped-up muscle car of the '60s and '70s. It made me feel cool.

Because of our age differences, all of us siblings got home from school at different times, and Mom spoiled each of us by making us what we wanted to eat when we got home. On Sundays, we all went to Our Redeemer Lutheran Church in Hancock. My brother, sisters, and I all attended until we were confirmed. Following church, we came home and enjoyed a traditional Sunday dinner of roast, mashed potatoes, and a vegetable as we sat down around the table together. The sad truth is that I looked forward to the meal much more than I did going to church. That's because even though we attended church regularly, I don't remember ever being introduced to the concept of a personal relationship with Jesus Christ. In fact, I didn't understand the need for a personal relationship with Christ until probably my last trip to prison in 2002, but I'll talk about that later in the book.

Some of my earliest memories related to going to church are actually sinful in nature. The church, like my school, was within walking distance. I remember a short period when my parents sent me off to church with my Sunday school offering. You could see the church from our back window, so I would walk straight to church and go in the front door, to make it look like I was going to Sunday school, just in case someone at home was watching. But then I headed out the back door, walked from the church into Stettner's grove, and came out about a block down, where I headed uptown to play pinball with my offering money at E & M (Elmer and Mary) Café. I'm sure God really appreciated that. Occasionally in my early teens, I would even steal the Mogen David communion wine from church. When I look back on it now, I see it as another example of me doing what I liked instead of what was right. Whether it was the offering or the wine, today I realize I was stealing what belonged to God and using it for my own sinful pleasure.

Our small, three-bedroom house sat on the curve about a half block from the water tower. That location offered a bird's-eye view of Main Street, which was about two blocks long. As a young child walking on that tarred street, I remember seeing the trees across the back of our yard covered in solid orange with migrating monarch butterflies. By 5:00 in the evening, you'd find me peering out the window or shooting baskets in the driveway as I watched for Dad to come home from work. I'd look beyond the large trees that lined the sidewalk along our street for the first glimpse of him. Dad walked that sidewalk most days to and from the post office where he worked as a postal clerk. When I spotted him, I'd run out the door and down the sidewalk. "Let's play horse," I'd beg, or I'd ask him to "watch my shot."

My father was a good man, about six foot tall and slender, with a full head of very white hair. Dad was a good athlete, but he never talked about it. Instead, I heard about it from other "old-timers" who said he was the best first baseman around. I checked it out in a 1941 yearbook and they were right. My father was a man of integrity and was liked by almost everyone. Even though he showed promise as an athlete, he gave all that up once he had a family. He never even mentioned it. I remember him umpiring one time; someone gave him a hard time about having a big nose, and he said that was the end of that too. He taught me to never lie, but I didn't do well at this.

Dad left for work about 5:30 in the morning almost every day, put in a long day, and was satisfied to live in our small home filled with typical 1960s furniture. I'm not trying to paint a picture of a perfect *Leave It To Beaver* kind of life. Mom and Dad often went for rides to hash out their feelings, to discuss problems regarding us kids and just life in general, but they did communicate and work together.

Since our house was older, Dad used his skills to make improvements that made it work for our family. Our floors were mostly linoleum and Mom kept them spotless. We had one modest bathroom, and with three sisters, you can imagine what that was like. My brother, Brad, and I shared a very small bedroom. Maybe I should call it a sleeping space above the stairs, because the room incorporated the stair structure. It created what we called the "high thing," which was perfect to use as a catchall and as a clotheshorse. It was a space four feet square and five feet high. Brad and I slept in bunk beds even when we were older, to save valuable space. My mother, now eighty-three, still lives very contentedly in that house. It is a very warm and comfortable place that all of my siblings and I still enjoy visiting to be spoiled by Mom's cooking.

Like I said, Brad was six years older than me, and by the

time I was twelve or thirteen, he worked at Bell's grocery store in town. Brad was popular and had tons of friends. He always had a job throughout high school, and he had no interest in sports. However, Brad always liked to hunt and fish, and he still does. He also liked nice cars and partying. He'd come in late after a night out and throw his pants on the "high thing." I'd listen until his breathing changed to the steady rhythm of deep sleep. It didn't take long, if he'd been drinking. I'd reach over from the top of my bunk and grab a couple of bucks from his pants pocket. Now that I'm writing this book, I guess I'll have to call him and see if knows that I did that. It might cost me a little money.

All in all, I guess you could say that I grew up in an average family. In fact, until I was about thirteen, my home life was pretty mellow. But our quiet, small-town life was shattered when my sister became pregnant. Because that was a long time ago, and this book is intended to lift people up and hurt no one, I only want to say to those who remember the situation that it was not as it seemed. Words can't convey how hard that was on my sister as well as on our entire family. Annette was forced to leave school throughout the pregnancy and had to give up the child when it was born. After this, she changed a lot and started to party more. As the little brother who wanted to protect her, I started hanging out with the older kids too.

About the same time, my oldest sister, Lynn, was diagnosed with a brain tumor. Lynn was much quieter and more well-mannered than me. She struggled with that brain tumor at such a young age and lived with health issues throughout most of her life. Fortunately she was able to live a somewhat normal life – she eventually married and had two beautiful children, Josh and Jennifer. But during her childhood, we spent a lot of time at St. Luke's Hospital in Fargo, North Dakota. Until then, I'd have to say alcohol wasn't a big deal, but I eventually learned that a few beers or a shot of whiskey seemed to take away the pains in life. It was really tough sitting in the cancer ward at such a young age and seeing all the people who were struggling with real-life challenges. I believe these situations were a large part of why I became a protector of "the less fortunate," as I called them. People who were not just right had an ally with me.

For example, Mike, the brother of Tammy, a classmate of mine, was terrified of school. He became relaxed and excited when he saw me as he rode his bike to school. Gemela, one of several mentally challenged adults who rode the bus to Morris with us as we went to carpenter class, provided me with one of my biggest lessons in life one day on our way to Morris. She would rock back and forth all the time, not making eye contact with anyone. One of my friends thought it would be funny to spit in her glove. I rebuked him and told my friends to treat these people special, to try it for just one week. We did, and within a week, these scared, lonely, vulnerable adults were happy to see us and to show us the pictures of Jesus they colored that day. On Friday, they would gleefully say, "No school tomorrow! No school tomorrow!" Little did I know at the time, that we were sharing the love of Christ and seeing for ourselves the power of that love.

Within this time period, I became the bat boy for the Hancock Orphans baseball team. The Orphans had a good ball team, but they were quite a bunch of drinkers. It was also probably the rowdiest and most harassing team in the league. There was almost a sort of competition to see who could come up with the best one-liner as we chattered. I would assume we were not a favorite in the league. I ended up sneaking beers, and this is part of how my drinking life began at the age of thirteen. I liked it, and it didn't take long before I was drinking with my other friends away from the Orphans too.

As youngsters, my friends and I often roamed the town and

had apple fights, snowball fights, and tomato fights, and not just with each other. We often launched our ammo of choice at cars from the top of a flat roof of one of the restaurants on Main Street. By the time I was fourteen, we added weed to the mix of our antics. My mischief grew more reckless and my pranks more radical. I remember Jerry, Steve, and I carrying a pizza to the top of the water tower. We got stoned up there and that was a mistake. It took a good while for us to convince ourselves to go back down.

One Sunday I wore the army jacket that my sister Annette had drawn a skull and crossbones on. I stood in the small entry of the drugstore on Main Street and patiently waited for the stream of cars to start coming up the street from the four churches located within a few blocks. I sprayed the arms of the coat with lighter fluid, lit them, and stepped out onto the sidewalk to freak out the passersby.

Sometimes we'd sneak beer or booze from friends' parents. It didn't come from our house though, because Mom and Dad seldom had booze in our home. Dad drank only occasionally, and when he did, he was actually quite funny. One time Mom was trying to be mad at Dad after a few too many. He lay down on the couch and pulled a rug over himself as a blanket. Mom could not keep from laughing. I'm sure he had a witty word to go with it too. You had to be there.

When my friends and I weren't doing something like that, we'd shoot some hoops. My friends and I often went down to Richard Schmidgall's house to play basketball. Richard was the father of kids I played ball with, and I think was president of Hancock Concrete at the time. All of the kids were younger than me, so I always brought some candy for them. They called me the candy man. We all loved basketball and would even shovel off the basketball court in the winter to play, until we figured out how to pick the lock for the "little gym." It wasn't too hard to get enough people to play.

At the age of thirteen, a bunch of my friends and I got mini bikes. It wasn't easy talking my dad into buying me the bike, especially when I backed up Dad's old '59 Ford work car with a three-speed into the tree to show off for my friends. I popped the clutch and had my driver-side door open. It hooked on a tree and bent all the way around. Being the body men we were, my friends and I tried to push it back and pound out the dents, to no avail. I had a hard time coming up with a good cover story, and with my mini bike on the line, I thought it best to just come clean about my "innocent" mistake. Of course, instead of a burnout, I said that "my foot slipped off the clutch."

Once I had the bike, my friends and I tore up the streets. It didn't go unnoticed. An article in the small local paper, the *Hancock Record*, said "they" needed to get us under control. By that time, I was feeling independent and self-reliant, but I had no clue I wasn't mature. I thought I was just having fun, but many of the choices I made were not good or wise. The truth was, that with each poor choice, I gradually walked further and further from the ethics my parents had tried to instill in me.

For instance, one time when a couple of friends and I walked into the alley behind the liquor store, we came across a dead cat. Being the pranksters we were, we hung the cat off some steps behind the bar. We thought it was funny, but a photo of the hanging cat was published in the paper the following week, making readers wonder who could be so cruel. It wasn't until the picture showed up in the paper that I realized that people actually thought that the cat had been murdered.

When I entered the seventh grade it was a big deal. In Hancock, kindergarten through twelfth grade all met in the same building, which consisted of an old, tall, brick building adjoined by a couple of longer, one-story buildings. Going into seventh grade meant I got to go to the old building where all the big guys were. I was elected class officer to represent our class in the seventh grade. It was a bittersweet time because of the things going on at home. One day as I was on the way to a school meeting, the principal made some unkind comments about my family. At age thirteen, his words hurt me a lot. The old adage that "sticks and stones will break my bones but words will never hurt me" is a lie from the pit of hell. (*The soothing tongue is a tree of life, but a perverse tongue crushes the spirit.* – Proverbs 15:4)

As if the raging hormones of the teen years weren't enough to deal with, the emotional issues with my sisters nudged me to the edge. The principal, this man I was supposed to respect, didn't deserve my respect, and I wasn't going to give it to him. Somewhere along the line, he acquired the nickname "Toad." It would show up written in bathrooms and in other places. Stuff like "Toad sucks." I remember one day him asking me who this Toad guy was.

It wasn't just me that was changing, though. Times were changing too. For instance, for the fourth of July, when I was about fourteen, the town held a street dance. Hancock knew how to throw great celebrations on July 4. The town swelled to a few thousand people. Crowds filled the streets, but most of them were hippies and mostly came in from neighboring towns. The crowds grew very rowdy and began throwing firecrackers and other fireworks at the police. I remember a guy from Benson grabbing the hat off John, our police chief, and running off with it. His son, Darrel, took off after the guy, only to be followed by more hippies. A while later Darrel came back empty-handed.

The hippies walked over to the fire station, put on some of the firemen's clothing, and jumped in a fire truck and drove off. I recognized these guys as some of the guys my sister and I had begun to hang around with. They drove through Howard

D's yard and ran over his swing set. I'll never forget it. It took Hancock a while to forget it too. They didn't have another dance for many years. At that age, I thought all that had happened was pretty cool.

I grew bolder in my own pranks too. For instance, one not-so-innocent prank involved a teacher's bike. I didn't really get along with this teacher, so with the help of some friends, we hoisted his bike up to the roof where he'd see it when he came to his first-hour class. We didn't just hijack the bike and misplace it; we made sure we vandalized the bike. When the teacher walked into class, kids were lined up at the window staring out onto the flat roof across from study hall at the bike he used to ride to school every day. The tire from that bike hung in the shop for a long time. It was supposed to bother the perpetrators, but it had little effect at the time. I am now sorry for what I did.

Don't get me wrong. I didn't live the life of a hooligan every moment of the day. In fact, I had my first real job in seventh grade, and it came about by what today would be called a random act of kindness. I rode my bicycle to a small dairy farm outside of town called the Da-Don farm. It was named after Dave and Don Joos. One day I found a calf with its front legs caught in the water trough. I pulled him out and thought I had saved his life. I ended up working for this dairy farmer all through high school till I graduated. We often went to horse shows to show horses or cow shows to show cows. I found it exciting and still look back at those times with fond memories.

My little sister, Lori, was kept under much more control than the rest of us. She played sports and lived a much more controlled life than Brad, Annette, and I. I think my parents saw where the rest of us were headed and hoped to save their youngest from following that path. I can hear Lori saying right now, "I couldn't do anything after you guys."

My parents did their best. I was close to both of them. My

father was my hero and my mother did everything for us. Mom always supported us and showed us love. To this day, she is the glue that holds our family together. She is eighty-three and looks like she will live to be a hundred! My parents raised us to be honest and good kids. I'm sorry to say, I didn't live up to their expectations, and my biggest regret in life is that my father, who did everything for me up to his very last years, was never able to see me get clean and sober. I attended his funeral flanked by prison guards, in 1999, and attended my sister Lynn's funeral in prison chains, in 2002. However, that's about the time Christ got hold of me and transfused me with new life ... His life. And what's really cool is that my two sisters, my mom, and my brother, Brad, are all Christians now. Everyone has a good life now and all are hard workers. My brother has been clean now himself for many years. My siblings are all married and we have a great extended family.

CHAPTER 2

Work on the Farm

*Whatever you do, work at it with all your
heart, as working for the Lord, not for
human masters.* (Colossians 3:23)

In junior high I started to work summers at the Da-Don farm,
which was just two miles north of town. In the beginning, I
rode my bike to the farm each day, until I talked my dad into
buying me that mini bike.

After that, I'd drive that mini bike the two miles north of
town to the farm, with the wind blowing my hair. I'd head
down Main Street, buzz down the hill, ride over the railroad
tracks and up the hill, take a right, and after a few blocks turn
onto the old Highway 9. That stretch of road was riddled with
potholes and was in terrible shape, but navigating the deep
potholes on the mini bike made it more of an adventure as I
drove by fields of corn and alfalfa.

The first time I ever had a brush with the law was riding home
from the farm on my mini bike. After the officer stopped me
for my offense, he followed me to the post office where my dad
worked. Dad was notified of my offense, but I don't remember
anything coming of it.

About halfway to the farm, a huge cottonwood tree stood
alone along the side of the road. It was just about the only tree
between town and the farm. I'd occasionally stop by the tree
and look around, and it was obvious others did the same. The

battered old tree's base was littered with beer bottles, food wrappers, and cigarette packs and butts. Other items of discarded trash lay within the shade of that tree.

Even though work at the farm could be hard, I enjoyed it. A white painted fence enclosed the large farmyard sprinkled with black walnut trees. I'd pull in to the horseshoe driveway and slow down on my mini bike to cross the three-inch pipes used at the gateways to keep the livestock from leaving the yard. The horses would walk up to the gate and see they would have to cross the pipe but would be afraid to.

The livestock on the farm consisted of milk cows, pigs, chickens, and horses. Back then, Davy and Donny were in the process of building a registered herd. Cattle were being bred with pure bloodlines for higher milk production with more butterfat and cattle value. Davy oversaw all the milking-related responsibilities and horse stuff, while Donny did the fieldwork and took care of the pigs. My specialty was helping wherever I was needed.

I'd arrive at the farm at 7:00 in the morning and find Davy already milking. By that time he had already fed the cows, because eating kept them calmer during milking. As they ate, the cattle would throw their feed around and scatter it, so the first thing I did was push the feed back into the trough and add some silage and ground corn. When milking was over, we'd turn the forty milking cows out to pasture while we cleaned the barn. I'd scrape down the gutters and fluff up the straw for the cows to lie on. Then I'd sweep up the barn before sprinkling lime on the floor to kill bacteria and keep odors under control.

During those hot Minnesota summers, the inside of the barn was often plagued with flies. Biting flies are a real irritation to cows, so we'd get rid of them by closing all the doors and fogging the barn with fly killer while the cows were out.

Thousands of dead flies littered the floor after the fog cleared and had to be cleaned up. That, of course, was one of my jobs.

Throughout the summer, we'd have other chores like baling hay and harvesting the crops. As I grew older I got better and better as I built muscle and strength. I threw a lot of bales of both straw and hay while I worked on the farm. Sometimes I'd be stuck in the loft and other times I got to ride the rack. Either way, I looked forward to the end of the day when Dave Joos Sr. would offer us a beer or two with home-canned tomato juice as we sat at the picnic table to reflect on our day.

On a typical morning, after chores, we'd go up to the main house where we all sat at the kitchen table together while Davy's mom cooked up the thinnest pancakes on earth, along with eggs and ham or other breakfast meat. Once our stomachs were full, it was back to our chores.

On summer days when we didn't have to bale or harvest, we'd spend time whitewashing the walls, painting the stanchions silver, and brushing down the cattle and washing their tails. When the milk cows came home, it always amazed me how each one went to its assigned stanchion. They always knew!

By mid-morning it was time to do the horse chores. I'd walk over to the small barn that held the horses and feed them hay and grain. Lunch was brought to the field and included a ham and tomato sandwich or a sweet roll topped with a slice of cheese. By the time I was in tenth and eleventh grade, we were rewarded with a beer or two, when the work was done.

One of the more interesting times of the year was when we would clean out the corncrib. Mr. Bolluyt would bring over his corn-sheller. We would empty the corn out of the crib and into the sheller to get shelled corn. When we neared the bottom of the crib, the rats living in it would start running out. The farm dog was a big St. Bernard by the name of Ben. He chased down many of the rats and that would be the end of that. At first it was kind of creepy, but I got used to it.

By about the tenth grade, part of my pay was to pick out a bull calf for myself. I chose a registered bull calf I called Amos. Amos had the run of the yard with the horses. Yes, I spoiled him like a pet, and he grew at a fast pace. I took Amos to cattle shows, and he was always the biggest in his class. In fact, he was so big the judges often questioned his actual birth date. I guess he must have eaten better than the others, no doubt. He was a good-looking bull, and I wouldn't let Davy cut off his horns because I thought, *What's a bull without horns?* Of course, I didn't quite understand how dangerous a bull with horns was at the time.

As much as I cared about Amos, by summer's end we parted ways when I sold him, so I could buy a 350 Honda motorcycle. It bothered me at first, and I missed him like you would a pet, but that didn't last long. Out of sight, out of mind, I guess. I had my bike. That's what I wanted. And I justified my actions by reminding myself, "That's what they do on a farm." Life became more and more about what I wanted or liked to do. I earned money doing other odd jobs, too, and started spending my money on booze and drugs.

I enjoyed the horses too. Like I said, Davy worked with the horses on the farm, and he really liked registered Appaloosas. Back then, he had a quarter horse stud named Cody, a quarter horse mare named Brandy Girl, and a prime show animal named Miss High Spots, who had almost-perfect white socks on all four legs, a white blaze, and a white blanket over her hindquarter. We took her to shows where she did well.

My favorite horse, though, was Spotanna, a very tall mare with a lopsided nose. One day, Davy told me he'd give me five dollars if I could ride that horse. She had never been ridden, and I was never one to shy away from a challenge like that. I pulled a bale of straw out to use as a stepping stool to mount her because she was so tall. I balanced on the bale beside her, jumped, and landed across her on my belly. She danced around a bit, agitated to have me riding across her back like that. Once she felt comfortable with that, I tied twine to each side of her halter to use as reins and came up with a plan.

While Spotanna watched, I grabbed a coffee can full of ground corn and let her into the corral. She eyed that corn as I dumped it into the food trough and led her to the far corner of the farmyard, where a pre-placed bale made it possible for me to hop onto her back. My plan worked just as I had hoped. Spotanna ignored the fact that I was on her back. The horse wanted that corn. With me on her back, she ran fast to that grain. I had to pull my legs in as we went through the gate so she didn't tear them off, but I won the bet!

A couple of days later I rode Spotanna again. I remember thinking I was pretty cool. When she walked under a tree I reached up and broke a branch off. Not the right move. A couple of horse bucks later I lay on the ground with the stick in my hand and found myself not quite as cool as I thought.

Throughout my early teenage years, I also enjoyed hunting and "plinking." Plinking was simply shooting at stuff. Many Sundays my dad would take me out to the dump by Page Lake and we would shoot some of the many rats that made the garbage and slabs of concrete their homes. One Sunday I actually found the stock and barrel of a single shot bolt action .22 caliber rifle. I picked it up and we took it home. It needed a firing pin and I had my first gun.

By the age of fifteen or so, I began to take the shotgun and walk out to Dutcher slough to see if I could get me a duck or a pheasant. Later, as I got into my junior and senior years, we would cruise out east of town, much as my sons who love to hunt do today. Often we would drive around and "burn one," meaning smoke a joint and probably drink a twelve-pack too. Hunting is yet another example of things addicts and alcoholics quit doing if it interferes with their using.

During those summer months, I still had to make it into town for summer ball games following a hard day of work. In Hancock, we started with peewees, moved up to midgets, and then moved on to VFW. I played all of them. And, like I mentioned, in junior high I became the batboy for the Hancock city team, the Orphans. I did this by being one of the kids who always hung around the park and showed I was eager to help out. It probably helped that Don Joos was the team manager too. My junior year I started playing for the Orphans. I continued to play until I was about thirty-three years old. That was when I went to prison the first time. Almost all our games were held on Sunday afternoons.

Baseball wasn't my only sport. In junior high, I started out thinking basketball players were all a bunch of wimps, so I wanted to be a wrestler. That didn't work out exactly as I had hoped. The wrestling coach, Mr. Wavers (who had never wrestled a day in his life), told me, "You don't have the competitiveness needed. You'll never make a wrestler." Now I had beaten a teammate in wrestle-offs (you wrestle someone in your weight class and the winner wrestles against the opposing team) who came from a wrestling family, but he wasn't going to let me wrestle.

My face grew hot with anger and I blurted out, "And you'll never make a coach!"

My outburst ended my brief attempt at wrestling. They kicked me off the team, and I decided to play basketball after all. But that wasn't as easy as it sounds, because even as a basketball player I had to sit out the rest of the seventh grade year on the bench. At our school, once you were kicked off a team, you were kicked off all teams for the year.

As a student, I don't remember ever taking a book home to

study. Instead, I tried to get my work done at school and depended on lectures to help me pass the class. It worked for me, but it isn't something I would recommend for others. Sometimes I wonder where I'd be today if I had applied myself, but I don't dwell on that. God has a plan for my life and today He uses me to help others like me find their way.

In eighth grade I started playing basketball, and by ninth grade, I not only started liking the game, but also started to take sports more seriously. Let's just say Mr. Wavers was absolutely wrong about my level of competitiveness. I practiced basketball almost every day. Like I mentioned earlier, we'd go shovel off the courts in the winter months so we could play, until we learned we could sneak into the gym to practice by picking the lock.

By tenth grade, our B team, which consisted of ninth and tenth graders, was very competitive, even as we scrimmaged the varsity. The good tenth grade players also had the opportunity to play for the varsity team, but you could only play five quarters a night at that time. That meant when the varsity coach put me and a couple of other guys from the B team on the A team roster, we'd end up sitting out a couple quarters of a B team game so they could save us for the A team. I didn't like that, so a couple of us went to my coach, Bill Richter, and told him we wanted to play on the B team if we were just going to sit on the A team bench. He listened to us and the B team ended up undefeated 18-0. A few of us did, however, dress for the varsity games and did get some playing time.

One of our biggest sports rivalries was with the team from Starbuck. As a sophomore, I went to a Starbuck girls' basketball game with a few of my friends. We snuck out of the game and drove to a secluded hill nearby and had some beers. While we were there, a bunch of trucks and cars from Starbuck drove up the hill kicking up a cloud of dust in the headlights. Who would have ever thought this quick trip to have a couple of beers would end in a confrontation with our arch rivals. The aggressive way they drove up didn't bode well. It didn't take long for us to be shouting insults at each other. Insults turned to threats, and it really got out of hand. My friends and I were badly outnumbered. One of my friends happened to have a .22 in his trunk that we used for shooting gophers and cans. He grabbed it and pointed it at the Starbuck gang. They said, "Ah, he's bluffing."

I snatched it from my friend and the Starbuck crowd backed up a few steps. "Foss has got it," one guy said. "He's nuts." The small crowd retreated somewhat. We put the gun away and a fistfight broke out between Dennis and a Starbuck guy. A short time later a highway patrol and city cop showed up. When they questioned us we said, "We didn't take the gun out of the case." But the guys from Starbuck had described it perfectly, right down to the sling. I don't know why, but somehow we never got in trouble for that episode.

I started playing on varsity as a junior and led the team in scoring and rebounding. Coach Peterson was proud of me. I remember him saying, "He's coming into his own." Little did he know where "living life my own" way was taking me. I began hanging around with older guys and started to drink and smoke pot with them on the weekends. It didn't take long for the partying to filter into the week too. During wrestling playoffs at University of Minnesota Morris, I drank some booze before going in to the wrestling meet. Earlier in the day, I had learned that a guy just a couple of years older than me had died due to complications from his diabetes. His name was Curtis B.

With my judgment impaired, I ended up going into the wrestlers' locker room and picking a fight with a Starbuck rival. The Starbuck coach and one of my teachers (the teacher whose bike I wrecked) spotted me and knew I was drunk. The next day they confronted me about it at school.

Coach Bill Richter was the principal at this time, and he

called me into the office. He glanced down at a paper on his desk. "Mark, Starbuck has filed a complaint ..." He looked up at me and I knew I was in real trouble. "... that you've been drinking. If you're innocent, I'll back you all the way. But if you're guilty and it's only found out after you continue playing, we'll have to forfeit all the games you played in."

I couldn't risk letting the team down more than I already had. I signed a form that said I was guilty. I was kicked out of sports for sixteen weeks, which included the basketball playoffs and summer baseball. Coach gave me a ride home to tell my dad. I was crushed and my parents were so disappointed. They deserved better than that. I went to the playoffs, but I didn't get to play. We won the first game, which was against Starbuck, and I felt some satisfaction, like retribution had been dished out.

In senior high, I was all-conference in baseball and captain of the football team. In basketball, I was the leading scorer in the whole conference, averaging about 24.5 points per game, and I was third in rebounding. I broke the Hancock season scoring record by 120 points. I had dreams of playing professional ball, but looking back at it, at six feet tall and being not that good of a ball handler, I was dreaming. But at the time I thought I was pretty good. I felt I could outshoot anybody!

Yeah, I thought I was hot stuff, and that translated to the cars I drove too. My first car was a 1967 Fury III. I took out a loan from the local Hancock State Bank and made payments from my farm work. During my senior year, I noticed a pretty Christian girl by the name of Lorrie. She was a couple of years younger than me, and athletic; other than that, she was everything I wasn't. She was valedictorian of her class, not a partier, and she knew Jesus. I started talking to her when I had the chance. Little did I know where this would lead.

Chapter 3

Small Town Life Is
What You Make It

*You do not realize now what I am doing, but
later you will understand.* (John 13:7)

To be honest, because of all the partying I did at that time
in my life, I can't remember things as clearly as I'd like.
I mention this because some of my story may be slanted to
the way I perceived things. However, the purpose for telling
my story is that I want to give hope to those of you who have
someone you love caught up in drugs, alcohol, or just plain
life issues apart from a relationship with Jesus or … maybe
it's you. You may be viewing things with a similarly slanted
perception. For example, I don't totally understand it, but sitting around and visiting with people in general was almost as
bad as going to the dentist, unless, of course, I was drinking or
doing drugs. I tell you this because I want you to understand
my darkened reasoning and to see that Christ loved me while I
was yet a sinner and He died for me (Romans 5:8). I didn't see
or know that people were praying for me; however, over time
those prayers were answered. With that said, this chapter offers
a quick overview of life after I graduated and when I was first
married. I won't go into all the details, because I want to spare
my family the pain that the past can dredge up.

After graduation, I took out another loan from the same
bank and bought a 1970 Torino GT with a 429 Cobra Jet motor.

This car was a very powerful and fast car. It probably was not the best car for a young man like me. I remember the day I bought it. Dad and I went to Willmar to car shop. We went to a particular lot and Dad, not thinking, said, "Look at this. It only has thirty-some thousand miles on it and it's very clean."

About that time a salesman walked up. "Oh yeah, that's quite the machine. That thing has a 429 Cobra jet engine." As I looked at the white car with the orange fluorescent stripe down the side, I grew excited. It had a black hood scoop. Needless to say, my dad tried to herd me away from that car, but I ended up driving it home. I dropped Dad off at home. Now I had the opportunity to see what it could really do. I drove out by the concrete plant and stopped at the stop sign. I checked for oncoming cars, and seeing it was clear, I floored it. The adrenaline shot through me like a bullet as smoke rolled off my tires. I should not have survived owning that car, as I drove very recklessly, but God had plans for me!

Upon graduation, I entered the National Guard, which I had joined as a junior in high school, and was sent off to Fort Leonard Wood, Missouri, for basic training, and later to Fort Sill, Oklahoma, for advanced individual training. When I finished boot camp and came back home, I started attending Willmar Junior College with hopes of playing basketball. I sabotaged my own dreams with my drinking, though. It caught up with me early on when I got two DUIs while driving my Torino. I lost my license and had to drop out of school because I couldn't get there. Life under my control was out of control.

I received a check from the National Guard and started working at Tradesman Homes, a prefab home company in Morris. Here I gained valuable carpentry experience, which served as my occupation for most of my life. Later, I even started my own company, Mark Foss Construction, after leaving prison in 2004. I kept the business till 2013, with my last project being the general contractor for our new office/housing unit at LifeRight Outreach, where people like me can learn to build better lives with Christ. But a lot happened before the Lord got me to that point.

I graduated from high school in '75 and Lorrie graduated in '77. She had caught my eye a year or so before I dared to approach her. I again began to think about Lorrie. I didn't follow up on meeting her because I figured she was way out of my league, and she was two years younger than me. Finally, one day I mustered the courage to ask her if she wanted a ride. To my surprise, she said yes.

We just drove around a bit, talked, and I dropped her off. She was a good girl ... the total opposite of me. Her entire family went to church, prayed before meals, and was active at church just about every time they opened the doors. Her grandparents loved God and were avid churchgoers too.

Lorrie and I didn't have deep discussions about God, but I could see the difference in her life by the way she treated people. Her life was a witness to God, and it was clear she loved Christ. I don't remember her ever talking badly about anyone, even me, when I mistreated her.

I, on the other hand, always believed there was a God, but it was just head knowledge. My belief didn't touch my heart, and I never pursued Christ. In my mind, Christians were very hypocritical, and I didn't really want anything to do with religion (still don't, but there's a difference). My soured feelings toward the church and Christians were tied to how my sisters had been treated when we were going through such a hard time. Not only did the people who called themselves Christians not show love and help my sisters through that very difficult time; they actually made fun of them! It made me lose faith in people.

Each Sunday, I'd sit in church and witness the same people come in late and walk to the front and take a seat. The way I saw it play out in my mind, they made their grand entrance late just so everyone knew they were there. But really, looking back at it now, I was one of those hypocrites too. For example, Lorrie and I attended church together while we were dating, but I did it for her, not for the Lord. First we went to the church she grew up in. It was a small country church, a Christian Reformed Church whose attendants mostly came from Holland. They are great people, but where I was in life, it seemed too boring for me. I could hardly wait to get home and get out of my church clothes.

Once we were married, we attended the church I grew up in, Our Redeemer Lutheran Church. I had been confirmed in that church, but the truth is, I only went to confirmation classes to be around the girls. As an adult it all held no real meaning for me, and I couldn't wait until I'd put in my church time so we could get out of there. After church, we'd spend time with Lorrie's family. We'd go to either her parents' house or her grandparents' farm, have lunch, and stay for a visit. Her parents and family were great people who gave me the benefit of the doubt for years.

I did enjoy going out to Lorrie's Grandpa and Grandma's old farmhouse. Lorrie's grandparents were retired, and while the wood-frame farmhouse was old, they kept it up nicely. They had a manicured yard and a very nice chicken barn that could actually have been lived in. Her grandparents always made me feel welcomed. They didn't even mind that I brought my German Shepherd, Jonas, along.

Dinner usually consisted of prayer followed by a large meal like a roast, mashed potatoes, and plenty of desserts, but then we'd sit around and visit. For me, this was about as boring as church, unless there was a Minnesota Twins or Vikings game on. Having the game on TV was like a reprieve from an afternoon of tedious conversation. I'm sure they knew how I felt, and yet they always treated me with respect and welcomed me warmly.

Without the effects of alcohol and drugs, my communication skills seemed bland.

While small-town life has its advantages, there wasn't much to do generally. Once Lorrie and I started to see each other, most of the time we spent together was at my baseball games or her basketball games. That was one thing we did have in common – we were both good athletes. She was very good at basketball and track and field – another thing that attracted me to her.

I still played baseball for the Orphans in the outfield, but fielding wasn't my strong suit. I wasn't fast, and so I didn't cover a lot of ground. What kept me in the lineup was my batting. I batted left-handed and I was a decent hitter … a pull hitter. After the games, the team always sat around and drank. Lorrie tried to hang out with us, and she put up with a lot, but often left to go home without me. I loved her and often told her how much she meant to me, but looking back on it now, I see that my actions didn't really match up with my words. I selfishly satisfied my desires to "feel good" and popped open another cold one and caught a buzz, even though I knew she would rather I didn't.

CHAPTER 4

Marriage Not So
Happily Ever After

Do not conform to the pattern of this world, but be transformed by the renewing of your mind. Then you will be able to test and approve what God's will is—his good, pleasing and perfect will. (Romans 12:2)

I lived the partying life, but in my mind at the time, I always tried to show Lorrie respect ... until we were married. Once we tied the knot, I began to take her for granted. Having a Christian woman as a wife meant she would not stray on me. Yet even though I believed that, I was still controlling and jealous. When I drank it was worse. I made her life a living nightmare on many levels. She turned heads wherever we went, and I actually put her in situations with my friends who drank. I never felt worthy of having such a beautiful woman, and when the people around me reinforced those feeling with comments like "What are you doing with him?" the jealousy came out.

On a very hot August day, in Our Redeemer Lutheran Church, I took Lorrie as my wife. It wasn't a huge wedding. I was twenty-one and she was nineteen. I sweated at the front of the church in my suit, as she walked the aisle in her long, white dress. We exchanged vows in front of a couple hundred people. After the standard reception, we had a party with a keg at a friend's house, and spent our wedding night nine miles away in a hotel in Morris.

After we were married, we attended the Lutheran church on Sundays and Lorrie played the organ. My thoughts about God hadn't changed. I knew about Him, but I didn't know Him. I guess you can say I was one of the hypocrites sitting in the pews pretending to be something I wasn't.

Lorrie was going to tech school in Alexandria, so we moved there. We drove an older car, and our very first home was a single-room apartment that was a real dump. The room was furnished with a bed surrounded by old, worn-out, second-hand furniture. It was a place for us to get by in while Lorrie started her second year of tech school. We rolled with it because we knew it was temporary, and only stayed there for a month until we could find something else. I was unemployed that first winter of our marriage, but collected unemployment, which helped make ends meet financially.

After a month or so, we found another place on Lake Darling at a resort. This was an awesome place. I'd drop Lorrie off at school in the morning, and I'd go home, go ice fishing, and smoke pot. At 3:00 p.m., I'd drive back to pick her up. When I did have work, I usually worked as a carpenter, but still suffered periods of unemployment. My drinking and drug use didn't let up, but I tried not to use drugs in Lorrie's presence.

When I had work, I was a good carpenter and a hard worker. Even when I was hung over, I put in a hard day's work. On those days, I felt miserable and thought about giving up drinking, but by the end of the day, I'd be feeling better and often went out drinking again. Sometimes to get through the day, I'd sneak a little pot now and then or snort a little coke, meth, or do some speed.

After Lorrie graduated tech school, we moved back to Hancock. She found a job as an accountant, and I worked off and on as a carpenter. We didn't have a lot of money, but were able to buy a house in Hancock in 1979. We got a contract for deed on it and only paid $20,000. It was a three-story house, but it wasn't big. It was an old farmhouse-style, wood frame, and had a one-step slab going into the house. I used my carpentry skills and framed up an entryway and added a double garage.

I took pride in our place, worked in the yard to keep it looking nice, painted the old shed, fixed the door, planted shrubbery, and made it look good. I spent a lot of time in the garage, and would smoke pot out there. From the garage, you could go down into the basement or walk up a couple of steps into the kitchen. The kitchen led to a good-size living room, with a stairway that led up to a couple of bedrooms. When we moved in we had our own furniture and, of course, a stereo with big speakers.

Right after we were married, Lorrie and I talked about starting a family. We tried to have children right from the start, but when it didn't happen, we gave up. We thought it was because of all my drug use, but we wanted kids badly enough that we finally got it checked out. It turned out that Lorrie had endometriosis, yet she had never complained about the pain. Once the problem was identified, the endometriosis was treated and we had two children. Derrick was born in 1990, and Brendon in 1992. True gifts from God!

My drinking and drugging continued to escalate throughout our marriage. I didn't really keep alcohol in the house, though. I was what you could call a bar guy. One night I went into a bar called the Back Door with some friends. We were tripping on acid and spotted some rivals from the nearby town of Herman. Words were exchanged, and one of my friends gave the finger to the biggest burly guy of the lot. The big guy charged my friend, and a fight started. The Herman guy thought he got the better of my friend, but my friend picked up a pool cue and smashed it across the big guy's face. Blood spurted everywhere and skirmishes broke out throughout the bar like a disturbed hornets' nest. The bartenders got involved, and the police were called. No one ended up in jail, but the guy ended up with a broken nose and needing dental work.

Around this time I met a man named Dean Peterson. Dean had purchased the local telephone company. Well, one night I was trying to make some calls, only to find that my phone had been disconnected. It's hard to sell drugs without a phone! This isn't how it was done in our small town. I had come home from the bar and was quite intoxicated. I went over to Dean's house and pounded on his door, telling him in not so nice a way he had better turn my phone back on. Little did I know that this man whom I despised (and he despised me) would one day be one of my best friends.

The bar where I hung out most was Grady's, partly because I had been kicked out of the Met Lounge for fighting. Grady's was known as the bar where the druggies hung out. We would drink, do drugs, talk smart, and play foosball. Foosball and meth were made for each other, or so I thought. We had leagues and tournaments. My goalie and partner was Terry. He was good! Sad to say, Terry is one of my many friends who ended his life while high on drugs. I have often felt the weight of what may have been my role in his life, as well as in other lives, which were tragically cut short.

Being from Hancock, we really didn't get along with the people from Morris all that well. However, in the fall, when the college students began to come to town, I became a Morrisinite. The football players liked to go to the bars and act tough. Naturally, I got to know some whom I made into customers and others whom I just liked to harass. One night I got into it with a couple of the football players out at the Back Door. This was a bar located at the Prairie Inn in Morris.

One time I brought a shotgun into the bar. When I was confronted, I put it back in my car, but the cops were called anyway. It was an old model 97 with a hammer, and so I told the cops it was an antique and I was just showing it off. No charges were pressed. Try that today! There were other times when things got heated and weapons were brought out. It's amazing that no one was ever hurt very bad, or even killed, as a lot of my friends carried guns.

Another night when I was all coked up, this friend of mine's brother was home on leave from the army. He had put money up on the pool table. I had put money up on the pool table too, and believed I was next. When the game finished we both raced to the coin slots to put the money in. A little shoving match ensued. I got my money in. When I put my hands on the table to rack the balls, he cold-cocked me and snapped my jaw. I knew something was wrong but went to a party and did more coke. I ignored the fact that the inside of my mouth was bleeding. Eventually, the blood I was swallowing caused me to pass me out. Lorrie came to get me, and I went to the hospital. I had my broken jaw wired shut for six weeks.

I was friends with the people who managed most of the bars I went to. I'd often close up the bar and go partying with these people. I remember one time we locked the door after closing, and I cut one huge line of cocaine the length of the bar and shouted for everyone to grab their straws. This created a little bit of a problem for me, as I had fronted (gotten on credit) the dope from a man named Michael Strange. He was a potentially dangerous guy, but I worked it out.

By this time I had many drug connections and gave a lot of drugs away. I often had drugs fronted, but I was often my own best customer and wasn't able to pay back. This led to me swinging some other dope deal to steal from Peter to pay Paul. As I sold drugs, my customer base, as well as my supplier list, continued to grow. Needless to say, I put myself in a lot of pre- carious positions with less-than-honest people. As I continued to drink and drug, I grew increasingly less predictable. A lot of people didn't care for me. I was not a nice person and would often get into fights. I was basically crazy. This was a defense mechanism I used to protect myself both on the streets and in prison. People tend to leave you alone if you act like a nut, and actually, it wasn't all an act. I was becoming more unstable all the time. Some people even called me "Wild Man."

It got so I would come home late every night, if I even came home at all. At times I was verbally abusive toward Lorrie after drinking. To say I was a terrible husband doesn't begin to cover it. Because I lost my driver's license in 1980, we didn't need two vehicles, but I still drove occasionally and was arrested for DWI on six occasions. I would often catch rides to other towns from people heading that way, or I would trade drugs with people to get where I wanted to go. One of those friends, Dave, has gone through the LifeRight program and now works for us.

As my drinking and drugging increased, I felt the need to go to bigger towns to acquire or sell drugs. A lot of my close drinking friends were falling away from me as I focused more and more on drugs. I smoked pot daily and did harder drugs often. Lorrie was nervous and worried when I came home drunk. Which husband would walk in the door? She never knew if I would be abusive or angry or would just go to bed.

I would sum up my marriage like this. I married a very special woman whom I loved dearly. After we were married, my addictions really took over my life. I no longer had respect for myself and would try to deflect blame to Lorrie or anyone else who tried to hold me accountable. There is no need to go into more specifics. You get the idea. I was a horrible husband and, for that matter, a severe addict. My reality was not in tune with the real world anymore. It was me against the world, society, and the police. I used that mentality to allow myself to continue on the road of destruction that was killing me.

I loved my two sons. My boys are very special men. Both well-liked, handsome, and intelligent. I tried to be a good father, but I was so deep into my addictions that my thinking was compromised and my values had diminished. Eventually, it was my love for Derrick and Brendon and a long prison sentence that helped me make a decision to live my life for Christ. He was my last chance.

Even with all I did, Lorrie never talked bad about me to the kids. She clung to the hope that I'd get straightened out. We prayed. I knew my life was a mess, but I hadn't bought into the God thing. I went to treatment the first time right about the time we got married. I lost my license in 1980, and didn't get it back until 2005. During that time, I had six DUIs. Overall, I tried treatment about nine times over twenty-five years for drugs and booze, but inside I figured, *why try. I can't do it anyway.* Lorrie stayed married to me in spite of my verbal abuse, infidelity, and drug use. She stuck with me through two trips to prison, many jail times for DWIs, and several treatments, hoping I would straighten out. Only when my boys were getting old enough to know what was going on did she courageously decide to divorce me, after fifteen years of marriage. By this time our kids were five and six.

I had come to grips with the fact that my marriage to Lorrie was over, and I moved into a house in Morris with a girl named Beth O. who was fifteen years younger than me. She was a good girl who never used drugs. We lived together for about five years. I was so pitiful; I told Lorrie if she wanted me to sign the divorce papers, she would have to give me five hundred dollars. I told her she could have everything except my tools and my stereo. Shortly after that Beth and I moved to Alexandria.

As I look back on my life while married to Lorrie, it is amazing how sketchy it is. I lived in such a constant state of inebriation, with days, weeks, and months running together, that I have a very hard time remembering what happened and when. I do remember several occasions where I almost gave up all hope of ever beating my addictions … but God! While I could dig up more information on the life I led then, it serves little purpose to dredge up things that were very painful for a lot of people and I prefer to focus on the hope Christ has to offer.

Since I have been clean (April 18, 2002), Lorrie and I have both attended almost every game our two sons have played in throughout high school and college. We have treated each other with respect and dignity. Lorrie never put me down to my two boys when things were tough. All she told them was that I had a problem. I am so thankful that she did that, because today I have a relationship with both of my boys, thanks to her. Lorrie's husband Gary also deserves credit for helping to raise my sons and provide for them when I wasn't able to.

CHAPTER 5

When My Luck Ran Out

*In all your ways submit to him, and he will
make your paths straight.* (Proverbs 3:6)

Alcoholism had really gotten ahold of me. Yes, I used drugs
regularly, but I drank every day. I can remember many
times sitting by myself feeling worthless and alone. I begged the
Lord to "fix me," but I wasn't ready. I had lost all self-respect.
It's at that point I believe people make a conscious effort to take
on the "it's me against the world" attitude, or admit failure. I
didn't like who I had become, but fell into thinking, *Why try,
I won't be able to change anyway.* Lie!!

I see how fortunate I was not to land in prison earlier than
I did. In 1989, my luck ran out. Just ten years after Lorrie and
I bought our house, I was arrested for the first time for selling
drugs. I was in my early thirties at the time and still married.
Instead of enjoying the blessing of life with my family, back
then I sold drugs out of a number of bars. I considered one
bar in Morris to be my "home" bar. As it turned out, the feds
learned it was my home bar too.

They sent in an undercover agent from the Bureau of Criminal
Apprehension to target me for selling drugs. The guy had a beard,
was rough looking, and drove an older Monte Carlo. I was a
little suspicious, but we started playing pool and bought each
other drinks. He asked about buying pot. I checked him out,
but he had a fake I.D. from one of the Dakotas, and according

to his cover, he was a truck driver. I sold him some pot against my better judgment.

Over time, he came and went, which fit with his cover. He'd be gone a week or two and come back and buy some drugs. The investigation lasted a year, and eventually I sold him some methamphetamine. He asked about buying a quarter ounce of cocaine. Again, something didn't sit right with me, but we agreed to meet in St. Cloud to do the transaction.

I brought two friends with me to make the delivery. A friend of mine from Hancock, Jim, was driving. Another friend, "Fat Boy," rode along in the back seat. (Fat Boy is also deceased.) At the last minute, because I just had a feeling something wasn't right, I changed the place where we were to exchange money to Sauk Centre. We pulled in to the truck stop. I scanned the parking lot. Something just didn't feel right. I didn't see the guy I was supposed to meet, and I breathed a little easier, relieved that he didn't show. Just as we got ready to pull out, another car pulled in. It was the guy.

Jim and I got out of our vehicle and I climbed into the front seat of the waiting car. Jim sat in the back seat. I decided not to have the drugs on me. Jim held them because I felt uncomfortable about the deal. We made the transaction. Once I had the money, Jim handed the drugs over. We exited the vehicle and got back into our car.

When we pulled out of the parking lot, a bunch of other cars left the lot behind us. We drove about a quarter mile and took a right on Highway 28. A highway patrol car sat there and pulled out in front of us. We spotted about six other unmarked cars behind us. The trap had us, and we knew it. Our only recourse was to throw the drugs in our possession out the window. We tossed cocaine rocks in chunks and tried to sprinkle them in a way that they couldn't be found by the cops. Eventually, we were forced to stop. When we did, the cops brandished their guns.

We climbed out of the car. Cold winter wind bit as we raised our arms. More than one cop yelled, "Get on the ground!" I lay face down on the frozen asphalt with my hands behind my head. Jim and Fat Boy did the same. Life as I had known it was coming to an end.

After they had us in custody, they took a couple of cars to go looking for evidence, like cocaine rocks or any other drugs we had thrown from the car. Fat Boy had stashed some coke down the back seat, and they found that. They took me to a jail in St. Cloud. It was an old-style jail with bars and big sliding doors that clanged. Everything was cold steel and concrete. I ended up doing six months in that jail, my first prison sentence.

In the St. Cloud jail, while waiting to be transferred to prison, I met a guy by the name of Joe Parish. He was a martial arts guy and full of tattoos. He and this big Native American were busted for burglary. The two of them didn't have any money, so I bought them a few canteen items, and Joe and I got to be friends. He practiced his martial arts skills by rolling up newspapers real tight around the ends of a three-foot piece of cloth from his bed sheets. Then, tearing small strips from his sheet and tying them around the rolled-up newspapers, he formed this into a pair of nunchucks to practice.

One weekend, Joe and I got transferred to a brand new jail in Long Prairie, Minnesota. We were housed in the maximum-security wing. Joe, being an ex-con, strategized on how to break out of this new jail from day one. He broke a steel leg brace off one of the tables, but kept the table propped up so no one noticed. He stood on the toilet, which was right next to the door, and used the brace to knock an opening in the ceiling. Gradually, a hole formed, but the guards didn't see it when they glanced into the cell because it was so close to the door. Debris sprinkled the floor, and he scooped it up and flushed it down the toilet. He also quit eating to get skinny enough to fit through the hole when it was big enough. This meant extra food for me, a treat in jail.

Joe chiseled away at the ceiling every chance he had. Eventually he hit metal mesh and pounded his way through it. After about two weeks, he could stand on his toilet and pull himself up into the ceiling. "I'm going to escape," he told me. When he wasn't working on the hole in the ceiling, he would stare out the window at the people coming to work and leaving. He was getting a plan down of which car to steal.

I learned I was being transferred in the next few days and said, "Don't do it until I get transferred." Otherwise, they'd know I knew and I'd get into more trouble. He agreed to wait. It wasn't long after I was transferred that I heard they caught a guy up in the ductwork. I knew it was Joe. My relationship with Joe turned out to be an important one as I made my way into the prison system.

Back then, smoking was still allowed in prison and cigarettes were used like money. That's how people dealt with things. If you were going to buy some hooch (homemade liquor) or pot, you'd often trade with cigarettes. Gambling was done with cigarettes. The weak people got extorted for cigarettes and canteen goods all the time. Prison is a ruthless dog-eat-dog environment.

It's worth mentioning that upon my very first time in prison I was assigned to a young woman as my parole agent. Her name was Julie E. Julie told me sometime after my second trip to prison that she "started her career with me and would probably retire with me."

I was transferred to Stillwater prison, the second-oldest high-security prison in Minnesota, built in 1910. (St. Cloud prison was built in about 1890.) The old block building was hidden from the world behind a wall lined with razor wire at the top, and it went twenty-some feet into the ground, so you couldn't dig your way out. Inside, the cells were arranged in long galleys about a block long, in four tiers stacked on top of each other. Across from the cells was a wall of little square windows that let light in, with some of the windows broken. I was assigned to be on the top tier, in the second cell from the corner in B-west, or a.k.a. the Wild, Wild West. I was the only white guy in there for about twenty cells. Because our cells were about as far as possible from 5-0 (what we called the police), it was a favorite place to do drugs. People on the tiers below would watch and warn anyone of approaching officers.

One of the most important times of the day in prison is mail call. Every day I, like everyone else, would listen for the boots of the officer coming down the galley to bring mail. It got to the point that you could tell by the speed of the officer's gait if you had mail or if he was just going to pass by. I was fortunate to get mail, but many inmates never got anything other than court papers. I always enjoyed the mail that told me how some people were saying I was a narc. I would tell them that it would probably be a lot more accurate to look at the people who got caught that never went to prison than the ones that did. Duh. Letters from family were encouraging, while the rare letter from a friend usually contained updates on lives being lost or destroyed.

We all called our cells our "houses." My neighbor was Keno Larson, a black gang member who had aspirations to be a pro boxer. Keno had the corner house. We kept an eye on each other's stuff when one of us was in the shower house or on the flag. The flag was a common area where there were metal-like picnic tables bolted to the floor where people could play cards, dominos, or whatever. The tables were bolted down like almost anything in prison that could be used as a possible weapon. Not that we owned much, but in prison you often bartered with your neighbors for canteen items like juice, a honey bun, or coffee. Someone would ask, "You got a pop?" If you did, you'd have to figure out how to slide it out of your cell and get it to them. We'd make a string from our sheets, or use a wire hanger to grab it with.

It was very expensive to get drugs into Stillwater. When I did get them, I'd go to a black guy I knew, and I'd have a friend of mine on the street meet a friend of his. When he got it smuggled in, I'd give him half, but there were times I wouldn't have any pot. Generally, the gangs in there have more access to drugs than most of the general population. A lot of the drugs were smuggled in by visitors, which required some real imagination, or a willing guard. My neighbor Keno wouldn't sell me any, but he'd lay a pinch on top of my TV and say, "Don't tell the brothers." He also liked making hooch, but I wasn't really into it because it tasted terrible. Plus, I didn't really like getting drunk in prison, though I accepted his offer out of courtesy and respect.

If you want to stay out of trouble in prison, the best thing to do is to just go to meals and spend most of your time in your house or maybe in the library. The key is to stay out of the main flow of the actual prison. Don't go to the yard. Just kind of seclude yourself. But of course, that wasn't my nature. So I went to the yard. I played basketball every day. In fact, I played all the sports.

When it came to the gangs, in the '80s, the PMB, which stood for Prison Motorcycle Brotherhood, was the primary white gang. But I didn't hook up with them. I preferred to stay an independent, just like on the outside. I played a lot of basketball, but eventually it got me into a bit of a bind. I was really good at basketball, and the prison had a team that played against the guards and others who came in from the outside. I was a starter and the only white guy on the team of about ten to twelve guys. They called me "Larry Byrd." A couple of the black guys on the team said, "We know you can shoot, Foss, but you'd better learn to play defense." My defense improved.

We also had intramural teams. This tall black guy, Isaac Brown, a.k.a. Dog Bone Brown, who was in for killing a police officer and is still in there today, started a team called Cons for Christ. He asked me if I wanted to play, and I said yes. I guess you could say I was using my talent for Christ and didn't even know it. In one game I scored sixty-three points. People watched these games and every once in a while we'd upset a good team. An all-white team called the Celtics asked me to play for them, but I had already committed to playing with Cons for Christ.

One time when we played the Celtics, it got kind of rough. A big guy pushed me. I threw the ball at him. Guards surrounded us and quelled the temper-driven exchange. In prison, you don't know whom you're messing with. Later, I found out the guy was in there for murder, but nothing ever came of it. I look back at it now and see how God watched over me whether I realized it at the time or not.

On a regular day, when there weren't scheduled games, we'd have games in the gym. I was picked by some black guys to play on their team. We were playing a Native American team. I was hot that day. A Native American guy sitting on the bleachers talked smack to me the whole game. He finally got on my nerves, and I told him to go f*** himself, not knowing he was a chief.

The game finished. When I headed toward the doors to leave the gym, a couple of natives stood in the door to meet me. The chief had put out a little bit of a hit on me. I walked past them without incident; it was time for us to go to our cells. When the horn sounded for us to be released for a meal, I went to my meal. When I came back to my cell, a couple of natives rolled in on me. All of a sudden being on the top tier turned out not to be the best place, if you're going to fight. I got punched. One of the guys pulled hair out of my head. I got a couple of punches in and sat back on my bunk after they left. *That was a little intense*, I thought. But it wasn't over. About half an hour later, it happened again, but this time three guys came in. They punched me a few more times. I got a few swings in, but their threats were getting bigger. "We're going to kill you," one guy whispered under his breath.

When they left, I slumped onto my bed and thought, *That's enough of this crap.* My friend Joe Parish had ended up coming to Stillwater and I went to talk with him. As a con he knew a lot of people and was hooked up. Lifers know who's who and who to talk to. It's prison politics. He told me to stay in my house and he walked away. Ten minutes later he came to my house and said, "It's been taken care of." To my surprise, I had a couple natives apologize to me, and I never had another issue with them. Actually, throughout most of my prison times I often hung out with Native Americans. Jason H. and Mike L. are good friends of mine even to this day.

Life in prison is more expensive than most people realize. Inmates are responsible for getting their own hygiene products, including things like deodorant, toothpaste, and a toothbrush. Items are never marked down or on sale. If anything, prices go up. For instance, you'd pay around eighteen dollars for a pair of gray sweatpants that might be ten dollars at Walmart. If you don't have any money, the prison provides some basics, but they aren't very nice.

I worked maintenance by fixing things like doorknobs, hanging hooks for clothes, putting up a chalkboard, and other odd jobs that earned me money I used at the canteen. I remember my very first day at work. We had only been at work about twenty minutes when the alarms went off. We were ordered to hit the floor. "Nobody move!" We were escorted to a common area. As we walked we were ushered by a puddle of blood. The guards checked each of our hands for any type of scrape or abrasions. They do this because if you get in a fight often there is a scrape on your knuckles. If I remember right, this guy had been hit with a pipe wrench. Often a shank or a "lock in a sock" was the weapon of choice.

Plus family and friends sent money from outside. The thing about outside money is that the state gets 10 percent in Minnesota. That means if someone sends two hundred dollars, the prison takes twenty dollars.

The prison knew if I got money, because they opened all mail before I ever got it. Even with that intrusion, mail was a big deal. It was always nice to get a letter and hear about life outside the prison walls. Some people never got letters or visits. I felt bad for them, but prison is full of people who have burned every bridge. The result is that people have basically written them off. I was more fortunate than that. Even though I'd gotten into a lot of trouble, I still had people who cared about me, and I still had contact with family.

I called my parents once a week, and my dad and Lorrie came to visit. Stillwater allowed face-to-face visits. That's how most drugs were brought in, but I didn't do that. People would get some popcorn or something and get a drink, and swallow some balloons filled with drugs to bring them back to their cells. There they'd throw them up or pick them out of the toilet.

My sisters came to visit too. They had to endure a lot in order to visit. Searches were pretty intense to make sure they weren't bringing anything in. Once they were in the visiting room, you could give a quick hug, but personal contact was limited. No holding hands or anything like that. Between the cameras monitoring us, and the guards standing around, we were being watched pretty well.

One time when my two sisters, Annette and Lori, came to see me, we had a good laugh. They told me that when they were checked with the wand, the alarm triggered. Annette said,

"They asked if I had underwear on. Why would they ask that?" At the time, it gave me a laugh.

I said to her, "They were saying *underwire*, not *underwear*."

While it was nice that they all wanted to see me, I wasn't big on getting visits. I didn't want people to see me in prison. I was actually ashamed. But even though I was ashamed of what I had become, when I got out, I fell back into my old routine and was arrested again for possession of meth.

CHAPTER 6

Bad Company

Walk with the wise and become wise, for a
companion of fools suffers harm. (Proverbs 13:20)

During my time in prison, I had gravitated toward people with like crimes. The guys I hung around with were other dope dealers, people who made dope, and thugs. I did this so that when I got released, I had an address book filled with other dope dealers' names and how to contact them. This enhanced my ability to buy and sell drugs again.

When I got back home, I returned to my old lifestyle, knowing I only had seven more months on parole. I took steps to stay out of trouble with my parole officer, Julie E., whom I had to see every two weeks. After a month or so, visits were cut to once a month. I took every opportunity to satisfy my addictions around those visits, because even though my probation stated I wasn't supposed to drink or do drugs, that's exactly what I did. I was high and wasted every chance I got. For a while, I managed to stay out of trouble. I would sneak around drinking, but I didn't do drugs like pot, which could stay in my system. Instead, my drugs of choice were out of my system in a couple of days.

I put myself in a lot of very dangerous situations. On one particular evening a friend of mine from Fergus Falls and I drove to the cities (Minneapolis–St. Paul) and went to "crack alley" or Lake Street. I was in between shipments and we were desperate to get high. We went to a corner where a lot of gang members were selling crack right on the street. When we were approached, we looked at the rocks. My partner, Greg, bit one and said it was junk. "Who has some real dope?" he asked. Another guy approached our car and said he had really good stuff at his house. I told the guy to jump in and we would give him a ride there. As Greg drove, I turned around to face the man and told him not to do anything stupid because I was ready. I had my hand in my pocket so as to show I would draw my gun if I had to. Only problem was, I didn't have a gun.

We drove to a crack house on the corner of Portland and Chicago, not a good place for two white guys in a nice car. I was wearing a very nice brown leather jacket and snakeskin boots. I had several thousand dollars in my pocket. Greg, originally from New York, was dressed similarly.

The man went into the house to return a few minutes later with some crack. Again, Greg bit the rock to see if it was hard or not. He told the man, "Get us some real dope or we're out of here." He again went in and the same scenario played out. The third time the man came out, he was followed by another man who was wearing a poncho, and had both hands hidden underneath it. I did not like the looks of this. There was no doubt in my mind the guy was packing heat. I told Greg, "I don't care if it's soap; buy it and let's get out of here." Praise God, we did and all was well. We proceeded to a bar where we broke the antenna off someone's car to fashion a pipe to smoke the crack.

I could write a whole book on crazy drug deals, but I don't want to give any impression of glorifying drug use in any way. To me, drugs are death and destruction, period! No one who uses drugs or alcohol will ever reach their full potential.

For money, I picked up carpenter work. I'd do that until my addiction made me miss work. Once I missed, I blew it off and relied on what I made selling drugs. Life slipped into a downhill spiral real fast. My marriage was over, and I had lost respect even for myself. I was a terrible father.

The next couple of years were probably the most unstable of my life. I had loaded guns all over the house. A lot of people knew I always had drugs and money. I acted crazy and almost dared someone to try to rob me. The act became reality. I had a big German Shepherd and a Black Lab that would warn me of anyone coming.

On one occasion, a man had made some lewd remarks to my then-girlfriend, Jackie. She told me. I called him up and told him to come out and get high. When he walked through the door, I backhanded him, grabbed him by the throat, and put a pistol to his head. I asked him if he wanted me to put him out of his misery. The news of this and a couple other situations where I was getting more violent and dangerous began to circulate around the drug world in Alexandria where I lived. People were very cautious in how they interacted with me.

My drug use was way overboard too. I spent hours hallucinating with extreme paranoia. By now, I was a full-fledged junkie. I'd shoot up some drugs and start mixing my next blast. We cooked crack and smoked it at the same time.

There were times when I contemplated suicide. I even sat in a bathtub one time with a pistol in my mouth thinking it would be easier to clean up that way. Wasn't that thoughtful of me?

I lived on a farm north of Nelson with Beth. She wasn't into drugs, so we didn't have much in common. I had met Beth at a bar in Morris, when she was twenty-one and I was thirty-six. She was a cute young girl and she just adored me. (I don't know why.) Shortly after we met, we moved in together and lived together for about five years. It was around that time that an old friend of mine whom I hadn't seen in years moved back to Morris. I saw Jackie at a friend's house and told her she should move in with me and she did. I told Beth she should find someone her own age who could give her a good life. She moved on, bless her soul.

Nelson was a small country town, and from there I ran back and forth to Hancock and Morris to do business. I had drugs FedEx'd to my house or a friend's house from California. I had another friend driving to Juarez, Mexico, to pick up cocaine.

I met a guy from California and I sold him some drugs. He bragged to me about how good the drugs were out in California. I said, "Why don't I give you some money and you go get some?" I gave him fourteen hundred dollars with the understanding he would mail me the drugs. We kept in contact, but then I lost touch after about a week. He got out there with old friends. He sent me some drugs, but they weren't really that good. At least ten days went by. I called, trying to get a hold of him at his girlfriend's place. He wasn't there, so I started talking to her about drugs. I told her what kind of deal I'd make with her. She was good friends with a lot of the guys who cooked dope (meth). So I wired her a couple thousand dollars from a casino and she turned around and sent four ounces of meth. She sent it via overnight twelve-hour delivery.

Of course, I had it sent to someone else's address. It was pretty much pure methamphetamine. I think she was probably doing favors for the people doing the "cooking." I never met her in person, but we did three or four of these deals together.

At the same time, I had that friend of mine bringing me almost pure cocaine from Juarez, Mexico. So I was really out there. At one point, Jackie and I stayed awake for fifty-two days. I know this because Jackie made the comment about when she had moved in and that we had been high every day. We napped here and there but never really slept. We drank sport shakes, ate something like a pack of brownies, and drank a lot of beer. I lost a lot of weight and got down to about 175.

I was going to swing another deal, so I had the girl in

California send another package to my friend Kevin. I went to Kevin's house. Kevin didn't know he was getting a package. "What time does the mailman come?" I asked.

"Why?" he asked.

"You're getting a package," I responded.

I told him to bring the package I had sent him to Hancock and he did. He pulled up next to me in front of the liquor store in Hancock and handed the package to Jackie. With the package in our possession, we headed over to a friend's house and started the process of cutting up and weighing. Unbeknownst to me, the night before, a guy I knew was walking home from the bar intoxicated. A cop picked him up and offered him a ride. He told the cop I was going to be in town with a bunch of drugs. The police told someone at the gas station to keep an eye out. They saw the exchange and what the guy had told them confirmed the deal.

We drove out east of town. When we arrived in Starbuck, I drove up the hill there and spotted two cop cars sitting on the side of the road. I went through the intersection and they pulled behind me. I knew something was up. I was being careful. I'd been through this enough. I was driving a Ford 1-ton with a sleeper compartment, a pickup bed, and a dually in back. It was a big rig with a 460 motor. As soon as I started out of the city limits they threw their pursuit lights on. I sped up and turned onto the first gravel road I came to.

For about the next twenty minutes I took them on a chase up and down gravel roads. I could see cop cars in every direction I looked. At the first curve I took, I threw a package of meth out of the truck. After that, I sprinkled it out. I had five or six ounces in the truck. I knew I'd get a long time if caught. I ripped baggies, tore them in pieces, and littered the roads with tiny bits I hoped would be impossible to find. I needed to keep driving long enough to get rid of the drugs. I came to one intersection and saw the cop stopped. I knew they had laid a spike strip across the road. I drove around them, but the road it led to was a dead end.

During this chase, Jackie screamed from the back about how I was driving. We were very high. One minute she laughed hysterically and the next minute she screamed. She said, "I think we're going to be on TV." A dozen cop cars surrounded us when we reached the lake, and we couldn't drive any further. They pulled up with guns leveled at us. I got out of the car, threw my jacket on the ground, and lay down. They pulled Jackie out from the sleeper on the other side.

This took place around February 24, 1998. I was arrested and charged with ten different citations which included some felonies.

We were hauled off to jail. I was charged with fleeing a police officer, reckless driving, driving under the influence of a controlled substance, possession, and other crimes. I had gotten rid of most of the drugs, but they located the first baggie I threw out, plus they found chunks of meth on the floorboards, floor, and seat, so I was also charged with possession of methamphetamine.

After they had me arrested, the task force raided my house in Nelson. They broke the door down and never fixed it. As a result, a lot of my stuff disappeared while I was locked up. People just helped themselves. The cops were looking for things like money-counting machines. They must have thought I was real big-time and that I was probably making the stuff.

With Jackie and me being in different parts of the jail, they were trying to get her to turn on me, but she said she never saw me do any drugs, and she stuck to her story. Our bail was set at $125,000. I kept talking to the task force, telling them how many people I dealt to, how many towns, how many people I could take down if they bailed us out. Finally, after a couple of weeks, they agreed to release us under several conditions:

I couldn't leave the nine-county area.

I had to stay in contact with them.

I couldn't use any drugs.

We renegotiated. "People know me," I explained. "If I don't use drugs they'll know something is up."

They agreed to no drug tests and more or less gave me permission to use drugs. Wow. Now I basically had permission to get high. To keep our agreement, I called the task force guy weekly. I told him it would take time, because people knew I had gotten busted. The guy overseeing my role in this plan would ask, "You make any deals?"

I'd just tell him, "No, they still don't trust me."

This went on for about eight weeks. The task force decided I wasn't trying to help them and called me in front of a judge to revoke my bail. The judge reviewed our agreement and asked, "Has he left the nine-county area?"

"No, not to our knowledge," said the agent.

"Has he been keeping in contact with you?"

"Yes, he has."

The judge pointed out the fact that I had fulfilled my part of the agreement and said, "I can't put him back in jail." This upset a lot of police and citizens around the area, as I was again in the bars doing the same old thing.

Needless to say, all I was doing was buying time before my inevitable sentence to prison would begin. I was a huge mess. It was while living there that I got a call from a friend in Morris that Terry had killed himself. It's hard to describe the feelings that ran through me. I understand how people get desensitized when tragedies begin to unfold around them on a regular basis. Terry was the second friend who had called me within hours of taking his life. I wondered if I had missed something.

A few days later many of us met up at a bar to attend his funeral. Most of us were high and had begun drinking; after all, that's how we honored a friend whom we partied with. What a sick view on life. The deaths of friends was mounting – would I be next?

CHAPTER 7

Prison, Take-Two

He will wipe every tear from their eyes.
There will be no more death' or mourning
or crying or pain, for the old order of things
has passed away." (Revelation 21:4)

So there I was headed to prison for the second time. Ten years had passed. My addictions had grown, and I was a stranger to myself. My personality had changed to the point of total unpredictability. I was dealing with more dangerous people who, like me, lived life on the edge.

One time, some people I was dealing with had me meet some others in Benson at the liquor store to pick up some drugs I had arranged to get. I gave them the money but felt suspicious. As soon as they left I tested the meth and found it to be "bunk" (very poor quality). I stormed out the door, but they were long gone. I drove back to Alexandria and picked up a pistol and drove to Willmar to confront my connection. Praise God, no one answered the door, as who knows what might have happened. Nothing good could have come out of that situation.

During this time in prison the most painful thing imaginable happened. My father died. You see, I loved my dad with all my heart. He was always there for me. Even at the age of seventy, I would call him in the middle of the night from wherever, and he would come get me and take me where I needed to go. I recognize now how I stole his joy for the last fifteen years or so of his life. He only wanted me to "make it." I'm sure many hours of his day were filled with worry and prayer that I would survive long enough to make it.

I remember sitting in my cell one night thinking, *I should call home*. This was very weird, as I generally called once a week and I had just called the night before. The feeling was strong, so I called. I tried several times without any luck. That concerned me, and I began to really wonder what was going on. It was night, after all, right? Mom and Dad were always home in the evenings. I went to lockdown never able to get through.

I was sitting in my cell about an hour later when I heard the guard approach my cell with his keys jingling in his hand. He said, "Foss."

I said, "Yeah?"

"You need to call your brother." A sense of dread enveloped me. For a guard to come unlock your cell after lockdown to make a call could only mean one thing – someone had died. I nervously dialed the number. Brad answered and told me Dad had died. He had gone out for supper, then came home, took the garbage out, sat down, and died. WOW!

I was overcome with emotion as I walked back to my cell. My cellmate, Garza, could tell by the look on my face something had happened. He asked, "What's up?" and I told him. He offered his condolences, and I crawled up on my bunk and stuffed my face into my pillow to muffle the sound of my crying. It's crazy, but in prison you try never to show any signs of vulnerability. Even kindness is considered a weakness, so you handle yourself with a hardness not even you can recognize.

My world had really turned upside down. The person I wanted most to see me make it was now gone. He was also my biggest cheerleader. You see, my father followed me in sports for years, giving me pointers and telling me to stay humble as

I got to be a real good basketball player. He taught me not to be a hot dog. He said, "Don't argue with officials." And I didn't.

My caseworker told me I would not be able to attend Dad's funeral, as he was going to be cremated and there was no body viewing. I told her that she was wrong. "Oh, I will be going," I told her, and I shot a kite off to my friend Dennis Benson, who by this time was a deputy commissioner with the State of Minnesota Department of Corrections.

Dennis was a farm boy who grew up a couple miles north of Hancock. Being a few years older than me, we knew each other, and he even roomed with my older brother for a time when they lived in Hopkins at "The Horn". Dennis had started as a caseworker in the prison system, and had worked his way up to warden of Oak Park Heights as well as Stillwater. He now had a lot of power in the system. In a way, it reminds me of how God put Esther in place as queen so she was in place when He needed to use her to save the Jews. God placed Dennis in this position at this time to help me and my family.

Dennis knew my father and everyone else in my family. He knew it was important that I attend the funeral. He arranged for my transport to the funeral and I was allowed to go. Dennis was such a blessing. He not only allowed me to go to the funeral, but also arranged for me to be unchained at the city limits. Dennis remains a good friend to this day.

We pulled up to Our Redeemer Lutheran Church where I had attended all my life. I walked into the small church with guards flanking me on each side. A sense of sorrow swept over me. The guards were dressed in their very white dress shirts, sporting Lino Lakes prison patches. It was humiliating. My time was very brief. I was able to meet with my family for a short time, but then I was forced to leave before the actual service started.

I glimpsed the backyard of Mom's house from the church as I got back into the vehicle. The ride "home" was somber. Driving past Page Lake on the way back flooded me with memories. Where did the young man go who used to walk from home out to Dutcher slough, gun in tote, to hunt ducks or pheasants? I would take the hike around the slough, through Stettner's ravine, and work my way to Page Lake to see if I could get me some action behind the cemetery. The beauty of this land I had so often taken for granted stunned me. You see, where I had been living was mostly walls and concrete and lots of people, many of whom you couldn't stand. It was my fault that I was there.

I ended up working in maintenance, which made it possible for me to go just about anywhere in the prison. If a friend wanted to pass a note to someone, I would get a pass to go to a unit to go fix a coat hook or some such job on the work order. I'd grab a screw gun and tool pouch, sign out, and take the message. That was worth a couple of bucks.

Because of my ability to go pretty much anywhere in prison, I was asked by a lot of people to bring notes or whatever to others. Along with this "freedom," I was fortunate to have connections with almost every gang in the system. I would make deals with the Hispanics because they always seemed to have the hot peppers; others had tobacco, some had meth, and so on. At one point I was asked to make weapons out of metal in the metal shop. I won't say whether I did or not.

Other things I did dealt with day-to-day living. For instance, if someone had earbuds and the wire was shorting out, I'd smuggle the wire to the electrical shop in maintenance and get it fixed for a fee. Working in maintenance got me outside, too, when we were dispatched to do mowing and yard maintenance.

The thing about prison is that the property you buy is clear, so you can see through it. Televisions are clear; fans and hot pots are clear. They do that so you can't have anything hidden inside them. They engrave your inmate identification number on each item. I'll probably remember my number for the rest of my life (#118961). They do room and cell searches to be sure all property belongs to you. When someone is leaving prison, they often try to sell or give away their things, but it's not allowed.

I did start attending church off and on in prison. It was okay, but church in prison is a place where a lot of guys from different parts of the prison go to meet. Many of the people attending are not there for the right reasons, just like the real world. I continued to struggle with Christianity because of the hypocritical aspect I saw of it. I didn't understand that a relationship with Jesus was waiting for me.

My addictions controlled me. Even in prison I had sources, but I had to be careful. I shared the pot I got with one or two guys. That was it. It was a challenge to get your hands on the stuff, and it was just as much of a challenge to find a way to smoke it. Sometimes we'd make a joint out of toilet paper. Other times we'd use a page from the Bible for rolling paper because the pages were thin. Then there was the problem of matches. Matches were so valuable that we'd tear paper matches in half so we could get two lights off one. Looking at it now, it's clear to see how every aspect of addiction controlled me and led to one reckless decision after another. (*Do not get drunk on wine, which leads to debauchery. Instead, be filled with the Spirit –* Ephesians 5:18.)

Prison is like a city in itself. My days were a lot alike except for weekends. The nights were all the same. When the doors slammed for the night, I was left alone to ponder my life, my future. Loneliness and regret set in. At these times I would seek the Lord for mercy, strength, and comfort. I began to watch Joel Osteen, who told me that in the eyes of God I was precious and chosen. He said, "I tell those of you hearing the lies to turn to Christ." The lies I was hearing were: *Why try, I won't be able to do it anyway,* or *I won't be able to have fun if I quit drugs.* What a joke! All this while slowly killing me and my desire to live.

During my second "bit" in prison many of my friends began dying. I remember seeing on the news how DEA agents had raided a farm east of Hancock and killed the suspect when he came out with a gun. This was a friend of mine named Rob. A short time later a friend of mine was found dead under a car that had apparently fallen on him. This was odd, as it was on a day he was supposed to go to court. Some didn't believe it was an accident. A friend of mine in Benson killed himself with a gunshot, and another friend in Alexandria died of an overdose. Another died in a murder-suicide and others died in accidents.

It was making me literally sick to see the wasted lives because of drugs and alcohol. I asked God why I was still alive. Some of the dead were men who had been loners I befriended. I thought I was doing them a favor in my own sick way by making them a part of something, a friend in the drug culture.

In all, I ended up doing only about twenty months in prison. Just enough time to lick my wounds and to broaden my drug base. The prison that was supposed to help rehabilitate me sent me out the door worse than when I came in.

A couple of friends of mine and I thought the whites looked weak in Lino Lakes, so we decided to start our own gang. It may not be wise to say what it was called. I will say that in my mind I wanted to use it to create a drug empire both in and out of prison. When my friends decided that in order to get the full "patch" you would have to kill a minority, I said that was stupid and walked away.

As my good friend and spiritual leader, Jay Jenson, would say, "I wasn't that good at being that bad." But God!!

CHAPTER 8

More Drugs, Drinking, and Bad Company

Do not be misled: "Bad company corrupts good character." (1 Corinthians 15:33)

When I got out of prison the second time, I lived in a trailer court. Dad was gone, my wife and family were gone, and so I moved in with a couple of friends, Dave and Nancy. We had two trailers. We lived in one of them and for the most part sold drugs out of the other one. And guess who had moved to Alexandria? Julie E. She was assigned as my parole agent again.

I partied real hard but did get a job working for a cement/concrete company out of Deer Creek, Minnesota. For this job, two other guys and I had to drive out to California. On the way, we were doing meth and drove straight through to a place called Stockton.

Our job out there was to build a scale at a shipping port. The first day it was raining, and the guy in charge told me I had the day off and to take the time to plan a little bit. My planning included finding a bar. I ended up at a place called the Captain's Anchor and started drinking. That was back in 2001, and at that time you had to go outside to smoke. The bar was quiet, except for some guys giving the waitress a bad time. There were also a couple of old-timer ex-biker types. They exchanged some heated words with the men harassing the waitress and then walked outside to smoke. I followed them outside into the bright California sunshine and told them, "If they give you problems, I've got your back." I walked back into the bar and told the waitress the same thing.

I was still there later that night when the barmaid's boyfriend came in. She introduced him to me and told him what I had done. One look at him and I was fully aware he was a Hell's Angel Nomad, as he proudly wore the colors. Nomads are bikers who can be dispersed to anywhere to "take care of business." The older guys whom I told I would cover their backs turned out to be retired bikers. One of those guys turned out to be my connection for meth out there in California. For the next two months, the Captain's Anchor was my hangout. They called me Minnesota Mark, as I had made the place my second home.

I went back to work the next day and brought a bunch of meth with me. I was out there for about two months and I hardly slept the whole time. I'd go to the bars at night, hang out and do meth, and go to work the next day. It was a cycle. During that time, one of the old biker dudes turned me on to some crack. I was hooked mentally and physically, and it got to the point that it became inconvenient for me to wait for him to be around to get crack. I went with some other guys to let the seller know I was the one really buying all the crack. This was a dangerous place to go for a bunch of white guys nobody knew. When we pulled up, they had some lookouts and it could have been trouble, but they had seen me a couple of times with the guy who usually did the buying and they cautiously trusted me.

I was high all the time, and after five or six weeks, just two weeks away from finishing the job, they fired me. In fact, I made them fire me, because if I quit, they wouldn't have to pay for my way home. So for those last two weeks after they fired me, I just sat in the bars. When the job finished up, I climbed in the truck to go back home with five other guys, and we were all doing meth. In Colorado, we got pulled over. It could have been bad, since we all had meth on us. I personally had a couple of ounces on me, but we had a registered driver with a clean record. The police checked his license and insurance, and we were on our way.

We drove to Minnesota, and I went right to Dave's house and started selling the meth I'd brought back from California. I went right back into my old ways as if I'd never left. My life consisted of bars, drinking, and drugs – both selling and doing them. This went on for a period of time, and I was pretty happy again, but that was about to change. This guy I knew who went by the name of Wolf got busted. He bought meth from me and was wearing a wire, but it wasn't just him. I was in deep in more ways than one, and it all worked against me at the same time.

For one thing, some younger guys were taking advantage of me, and I went to their apartment complex and made some threats. I had someone else knock on the door and I stood around the corner. When they opened the door, I burst in and slapped one of them, grabbing him by the throat. I told them I wouldn't put up with the disrespect they were showing me. Now looking back, I think these guys were working with Wolf. They purchased more drugs from me, about three grams, but when it all went down, they told the authorities they had bought only one gram. They were playing both sides.

A friend of mine whom I hadn't seen for a while came back to Alexandria. Terry had a trailer in a different trailer court, as well as did my friend Jay. (Jay died of an overdose.) I hung out around there for a while. I had brought Terry with me to Willmar a few times when I was swinging some deals, and now he had decided to bypass me and go straight to my connection.

About this time, I was introduced to another biker, Wild Man. I thought the name somewhat funny since it was the same thing a lot of people called me. He gave me four thousand dollars to get him some drugs. I did, and he offered to help me get some pure cocaine down in the cities.

We drove to Minneapolis–St. Paul, and when we came back, I smoked crack all night at the trailer. My friend Terry was going to the Holiday Inn to meet my connection, and that night they got raided. Five people were arrested, but I wasn't with them.

At this time, I had a relationship with a woman who worked at the courthouse as a cleaning woman. When she went in to clean some of the offices, she found out there was a warrant out on me and gave me a heads-up. It seemed that the agents had already had me listed as one of the people whom they were busting that night in the Holiday Inn. Since I knew there was a warrant, I hid the drugs in the drop ceiling, under the trashcan liner, and in other places so I didn't have them on me, but they were still in close proximity. Just to be safe, I hid all the dope I had, but I was very intoxicated. When leaving the Depot Bar I saw two cop cars, a local and a highway patrol. I walked up to them and asked, "Are you looking for me?"

"Don't think so," they said.

I walked off and got about forty or fifty yards away, just enough time for them to call to see if there was a warrant out, and they changed their minds. They came after me and slapped the cuffs on and arrested me. I posted bail and shortly after that I was back doing my thing as if nothing had happened. But the consequences were hanging in my future ready to drop.

I stayed out of jail for a while as my case worked its way through the court system, until April 18, 2002. My mom and sister Lori took me to court that day. They waited to take me home. I knew I was looking at doing some time, but I thought the courts would give me time to get things taken care of at home between sentencing and serving my time. To my surprise, when they sentenced me, it was immediate. Because my sentence was almost eight years, they took me into custody instantly. I hugged Mom and Lori, said good-bye, and was put in cuffs and hauled away directly to the Douglas County jail. I was sick of it!

CHAPTER 9

A Cry to the Lord

After the earthquake came a fire …. After the
fire came a gentle whisper. (1 Kings 19:12)

I spent about two days in that jail, and then Steve Sibel, the
jail administrator, transported me to the state penitentiary.
It was harder this time. My sons were young, ten and eleven
years old. I was looking at ninety-four months behind bars. I
thought, *I'm going to miss their junior high years.* I loved my
kids, and I felt like a total failure. I hated what I was. I came to
the end of myself. I knew it was either die or fight for my life.

After talking Steve into one last cigarette before we hit the
road, the reality of a long stretch in prison hit fast. It was only
a day or so and I found myself with my hands chained to the
chain around my waist and to the shackles on my feet. I wished
this nightmare was over. I looked at Steve through the cage
that separated us.

As the transport rolled down the road taking me to prison
again, I told Steve I was done. I cried out to the Lord and said,
"Lord, You need to take this from me. I can't do this anymore."
I totally surrendered my life to Christ and asked Him to get
me through this. I knew this was it. I could feel the power of
Christ wash over me. I knew this time I would make it or die
trying. It was different this time. I knew my way wasn't working. I wasn't asking Him to get me out of trouble so I could
go back to doing what I always did. I was asking Him to take

control. From that moment forward, my goal was to live a new life with Christ at the helm.

The ride there is a blur. The trees, landmarks, and cities I knew all too well didn't even register. I was on a mission to save my life and be the father I knew I could be. I spent time in prayer and speaking victory into my life. My hating to lose (to a fault) was now my biggest ally.

I arrived at the prison and was the first person to go through the new intake system at St. Cloud State Penitentiary. I was put into D-hall until they decided which prison I was going to go to. I reached out to my friend Dennis B. who was now the deputy commissioner. He recognized that this was probably my last chance or I was probably going to die.

Dennis again made a decision about how best to help me. This time he said, "No easy roads." He was sending me straight into Atlantis, the drug program in Stillwater. I was awakened in the middle of the night and transferred to Stillwater … a closed-custody security prison. Dennis had me put right into a program called the Atlantis Chemical Dependency Program. When I got to this prison, it was run by a black man by the name of Bill. During the interview he said, "This has never happened before." What he meant was, while there was a waiting list to get into the program, I had just jumped ahead of everyone and was admitted into the program.

I started reading the Bible. I prayed all the time and I cried out to the Lord often. I always knew there was a God, but before this, I didn't have a relationship with Him. It was the difference between knowing about God and actually knowing Him.

When I was going through this program, it forced me to look at my life and to actually write my life story and read it to the group. When I got to the part about my dad, and going to his funeral in chains, and the guards walking on each side of me, I would break down. I couldn't go any further. The next time

I tried to read it, I broke down again. This went on for about two weeks. I had never grieved. Eventually, I got through it.

I started to go to church and continued to read my Bible every chance I got. The guards didn't know how to treat me, because they knew I was friends with their boss, Dennis. They didn't know if they should be harder on me, less hard on me, or what.

According to the program handbook, at a certain point in the program you were supposed to get privileges, but only a couple of guys were getting the privileges listed in the handbook. I brought it to the officers' attention and asked them why, since I had gotten to that certain point by now. Why wasn't I receiving the privileges stated in the handbook? I said, "If you don't make it right, I'll take it to my friend Dennis."

This made them very mad. They called me in for a conference and said they were kicking me out of the program and putting me into population. This is a term used to describe when you are housed with the majority of the other inmates. Normally that would have been fine, but Stillwater is a tense and sometimes violent place. I was worried I would get in a fight and lose the opportunity to go to CIP (Challenge Incarceration Program) boot camp, which is an intensive, highly structured, and disciplined program for drug and property offenders.

"You think Dennis will be happy with that?" I asked. They said they would discuss it and get back to me the next day. It was obvious that my newfound walk with Christ didn't just make my personal defects disappear, as my proclivity toward manipulation was working just fine.

They transferred me to another facility called Moose Lake. It houses a lot of sex offenders and most of the men were waiting to be transferred to CIP. I applied to get into CIP and was accepted and put on a waiting list. At that time the CIP only held between sixty and ninety guys. Going through the program shortened your time, so there was a high demand to get in. I think I waited about ten months.

During that time, the nightmare scenario of a death in the family happened again. This time my sister Lynn died. I was transported to Lynn's funeral in my orange jumpsuit and chains. This trip was different for me. My friend Dennis was out of the country on vacation this time. I wore my chains the whole time, and I wasn't given any time to visit with family. It is so very difficult to be in such emotional pain with no one to share it with, no one to lean on.

I would have loved to have had the opportunity to share my new outlook on life with Christ with my family, but was not able to do so. I'm sure that my being chained up in orange added to my family's grief. When I was being escorted back to the car for transport, the guards spotted my other two sisters, Annette and Lori, standing at a distance crying. The guards asked if they were family. I said yes, and they were allowed to approach and give me a brief hug, then off to prison again.

Once back in prison I stayed in touch by letters. Here is a letter I wrote to my sister Annette and her family, which offers insight into my life at that time:

> Thanks for the letter and card. Here's the deal. I blame absolutely <u>no one</u> for my life struggles. I used drugs because I liked doing drugs. Eventually, I became addicted. I've been to treatment numerous times and have always returned to using. I am not stupid (I don't think), but I was always willing to risk my freedom, and as it turns out, my health, for the quick money and fast lifestyle.
>
> I wouldn't trade my life with anyone's. This is not to say that I'm proud of it or happy about it, but I am a firm

believer that our individual uniqueness is a treasure. I cannot permit myself to feel sorry for myself while young children with leukemia and like diseases struggle for life. Many others suffer worse than me.

Life is rolling by now at a fast pace. Jerry Eide has visited me with Dennis and has even offered me the chance to come stay on his ranch in Montana when I get out, if I want to – to help me get my feet on the ground. I used to go out with his stepdaughter, Anne Stahn. She is a criminal environmental inspector for Minneapolis. Basically, clean air. Jerry works for Harvest States and travels all over the country. The main office is in Minneapolis.

Anyway, Anne used to be on drugs too. She's clean now, four years. She's had some poor relationships and has come to visit me the past two weekends. She has really brightened up my time. She's a sweetheart.

I wrote Mom and told her that my hepatitis C is getting kind of bad. It's a little scary, as I don't really know where I stand. I only know that it's got potential right now to be quite serious. In February, I'll have more tests done and I may have to choose between boot camp and a lot quicker freedom, or a $26,000 treatment that only works about 35 percent of the time and has severe side effects. This is what drugs did to me. Most people in my situation would panic or be very stressed out. I'm not. What will be, will be. I think God has plans for me yet, so I think I'll be around a while. If I wouldn't have been told by the doctors the results of my last blood tests, I would still think I was in good shape, as I feel good.

I won the prison free-throw tournament on Martin Luther King Jr. Day. Wow! Five dollars and my picture taken. Not bad, out of about 950 guys here. Probably 50 entered.

About my health, a friend of mine had Hepatitis C and the treatment worked for him. He said he would cry toward the end of the treatment. Some people die from the treatment and some commit suicide – it puts you into a deep depression. For me, if I have to do it to try to save my life, I will. The only other thing is a transplant (liver) and that's not likely. It could lay dormant for years too, and maybe just flare up.

My intentions of telling Mom was only so you guys knew what was going on. I've kept it quiet for a couple of months, but I thought in case something happened someone had to know. I don't want Mom worrying, as I don't waste my time worrying about it either.

Here's what I want to do: Do boot camp in July and be out by next January. Then pursue treatment or possibly an alternative to it such as herbs, vitamins, etc.

So why should I get another chance? Freddy is dead; Craig K., my partner, is gone; Rob E. – feds shot him; Rick L., Dan A., and Gary M. – drugs and car accidents; Dean W. and Joe J. – drugs; Stubby and Kevin M. – suicide. I've lost a lot of friends to this evil. Us lucky ones are locked up. Sounds good!

Anyway, I'm 280 days clean and sober. I think of drugs every day, but I no longer physically crave them. I plan on making it this time or why would I stay straight right now? I could use.

Say hi to all and explain what I've told you to them. I chose to do what I've done and it has cost me a lot, but the blame lies with me and me alone. I've hurt all of you and for that, I'm sorry.

I think I'm going to make it! Both physically and in life. My training is near its end. It's time I help others. I've been thinking about starting a youth center with messages to help kids with all sorts of problems.

I may write a book. I've been taking notes and I know a lot of very interesting people – some who are doing life sentences but are free on the inside.

Time is going by pretty fast. I stay busy doing some carpenter work, playing basketball and cards, and working out.

You, too, are all in my prayers. I'm fortunate to still have people who care for me in spite of myself. It's all good!

Take care
Don't worry
Be happy
I am

God bless.
Love,
Mark

I stayed away from the guys who did drugs and cigarettes, but I still did my little tricks in maintenance. There was some tension between a lot of the gangs at the time and I was approached by some friends who needed some shanks (knives) made. Because I had access to the metal shop and steel bandsaws, I risked it and helped them. Thank God, I didn't get caught. I played a lot of sports, including basketball and softball; I continued to read the Bible; and I watched Christian shows on TV. I didn't go to church so much, because most of the inmates who attended just used it as a rendezvous point for other reasons.

I actually wrote letters to my probation officer, Julie E., and to the courts, telling them I was done with that life and that they would never see me again. Since that day in the back of that cop car, when I gave my life to Christ, April 18, 2002, I have never used drugs or alcohol. To my surprise, I don't miss those things even a little bit.

I look back over my life and see God's hand, even before that day in April 2002. Remember that Julie E. was my probation officer from the beginning, since my first time in real trouble with a felony. And as God worked it out, she was my probation officer from my time in Morris in 1989 to Alexandria in 1995. She told me once about how one day when she was driving with her kids in Alexandria that I ran across the street in front of her car. She sighed, and told her kids I was a very sick man. She ended up moving to Alexandria, and when I got in trouble in 1999, I had her as my probation agent, again. She said, "I started my career with you and I think I'm going to retire my career with you."

I think she was right, as we are on the same team now, and we often work together. I have come to know many probation officers over the years and understand their frustration as they are lied to and deceived over and over again. In reality, they have to protect the public, but there is probably no one happier than them when someone truly changes their life and makes it.

CHAPTER 10

Challenge Incarceration Program Boot Camp

If someone slaps you on one cheek, turn to them the other also. If someone takes your coat, do not withhold your shirt from them. (Luke 6:29)

I was on the waiting list trying to stay out of trouble, and I finally got the date when I was going to leave for boot camp. When word got out that I would be leaving soon, I was approached by Shorty, a gang member, who said he wanted my wooden desk out of my room. I said, "You can't have that; there are cameras all over."

He threatened me. "You give me that desk or I'm going to trick off your boot camp." Translation: If I didn't do what he wanted, he would start a fight with me. You see, if you get in a fight, you're out of the program. It doesn't matter who started it. You both go to the hole.

I had to go tell my friends what he told me. One of my guys beat him up. My friend had bite marks on his stomach and a chunk bitten out of his arm. Now, this got things stirred up and other gang members came to me and said, "Come on, Foss, we need to go for a walk." We went out in the yard and walked some laps. I told the men what Shorty had said and they squashed it (term for resolving something without violence). My ability to play basketball at a high level definitely was a plus, as it did enable me to gain respect from a lot of people. In today's

Minnesota prisons, inmates are held primarily in a living unit with several hundred others. Because of that, you get to know most people. You learn how to read people.

The night before leaving for boot camp was like the night before deer hunting. I was filled with excitement and anticipation, which made for a mostly sleepless night. Up early the next morning, I greeted all my friends and said my good-byes. Most of them I have never heard from again. I left knowing my buddy who got in the fight for my benefit was in the hole and possibly looking at extra time. Finally, the call came. "Foss #118961, report for transfer."

The anticipation of heading off to this camp, knowing it would be tough, made me a little nervous. I had seen others who had gone to boot camp return because they did something wrong. Infractions ranged from getting into fights to giving someone a piece of candy. You are not to share anything with anyone. Candy in boot camp was limited to flavored cough drops.

I was loaded up on a bus with about thirty other guys. When you're in prison, you own next to nothing, so all we carried with us was a shoebox of stuff that included our toothbrush and toiletries. We were headed off to CIP boot camp, which was located about twenty miles up the road from Moose Lake. I watched the scenery blur past my window, and when we pulled into the boot camp complex, it looked nothing like a prison. It had no wall, no razor wire. Instead, it was a smattering of buildings including a brick office building, barracks, a parking lot, and a sidewalk with a yellow line on it, all tucked into the middle of a forest. It offered a sense of freedom I hadn't felt in a long time. I spotted ravens in the trees and thought about how different they were from the crows we had back home. It was a peaceful setting. Or so I thought.

The bus's air brakes hissed and the bus came to a stop. Some guys in fresh, crisp uniforms walked up to the bus at a quick pace and started screaming at us. "Get off the bus and get on that yellow line!" The peaceful setting shattered with reality. I started shuffling off the bus with my shoebox under my arm.

"No walking!" one of the uniforms yelled.

"You won't be walking anymore!" another of the officers barked.

I didn't know what they expected. I couldn't walk through the guy in front of me. My foot barely hit the pavement as I stepped off the bus when they shouted, "Line up on the yellow line!" They ordered us to set our shoeboxes on the line painted on the sidewalk. I didn't do it to their liking. They made it very clear they were in charge. When they told you to get on the line, you couldn't just touch the yellow line; you had to be *on* it. And I learned real quickly that you had to be looking at them. There was no doubt; I was in a different world.

In many ways, this program was like being in the military. They shaved our heads and assigned us to squad leaders. Mine was a guy by the name of Sergeant Cook. We were given typical brownish khaki uniforms with a baseball hat that was brown, blue, or red. It turned out that the different colored hats meant something. They started us out with a brown hat, which identified us as new, and we gradually earned a different color. When you're new, you have very few privileges. As you participated in the program, you earned privileges along the way. However, even when you did earn them, you didn't get a lot. Privileges were small things like a little more free time so you could go walk the track, but really, for those of us who had spent time in prison, that was a privilege.

We were assigned to barracks lined with bunks set up in rows side by side with a top and bottom bunk. I started off with a top bunk. I thought that was a bunch of crap, because at forty-seven years old, I was an older guy. That turned out to be the least of my worries. Things were pretty much run military-style. The bed had to be made just perfect. My socks and underwear had to be rolled up just perfect. If something wasn't textbook, they'd dump it out or tear up your bed and you'd have to redo it until it was done right.

In the chow hall, we all had to go through the line, get our food, and sit at a metal picnic table. The only person you were allowed to talk to was the person serving your food. Inmates did not talk to one another outside the barracks. There was an older woman who sometimes made bread pudding. She knew it was a treat for us, but we didn't have much time to enjoy anything we ate. We were told, "If you can taste your food, you're probably taking too long." I had about five minutes to eat my whole meal. We wolfed down our food in silence, except for the scraping of utensils against our trays.

Mornings started first-thing with calisthenics. We started with forty-five minutes of aerobic exercise. Like I said, I was forty-seven years old by this time, which made aerobic exercise really hard. On the plus side, I saw some guys lose forty, fifty, and sixty pounds. By the time they got out, they looked like a different person and as much as I didn't like it, it whipped me back into shape and taught me discipline I hadn't practiced in a long time.

After exercise, we'd go back and get cleaned up. We had about a minute to shower, maybe two minutes max, and the water was pretty cold most of the time. It gave you just enough time to get the sweat off and that was it. Everything was hurried; no matter the activity, you had only a short time to get ready for the next thing on the schedule.

After the quick shower, we'd go eat breakfast. That was followed by various classes for people who needed to improve their education. I tested out of everything, so because I knew enough, I didn't need to take any classes. Plus, because I had attended treatment in Stillwater, I was not mandated to take part in the treatment programs offered.

They had to put me somewhere, so instead of schooling, they put me in charge of laundry. I got a few extra perks like better socks and underwear with the job, which I considered a blessing. And because I ended up having more free time than others, I was kind of a gopher for the drill sergeants. A lot more went into the day's activities, but this gives you an idea of how they had my day scheduled for me almost down to the minute. Especially that first day! It was the worst. They eased up a little the second day, but life in CIP was very structured and intensive.

They had a canteen there, but you could only buy a few limited items. It wasn't like the canteen in prison. There was no candy. In fact, there weren't any food items at all, other than cough drops. So they became our candy. Instead, things you could buy included hygiene items like cotton swabs. However, no matter what you had, you weren't allowed to share anything with anyone. And when I say nothing, I mean absolutely nothing. I saw a guy get sent back to prison for sharing a cough drop.

It took almost nothing to get sent back to prison. You'd see some guys being sent back for raising their voice. It was pretty intense because there was a lot at stake. To make it through this program at that time, having a ninety-four-month sentence meant you'd do about two-thirds of your time. So it brought it down from five years to two and a half years. That's a big difference. The thing that makes it really difficult is that you're in such close quarters with people who are still going through rough situations with people on the outside, and no one has an avenue to display their frustrations without getting kicked out. Plus, frustrations mounted with the highly structured environment. Often, when you didn't do things exactly the way they wanted, they'd tell you to drop and give them twenty pushups. I did twenty for having my ID on crooked, for forgetting to take my cap off when I went indoors, and for other such things. Let's just say we all did a lot of pushups.

We had to do chores there like lawn work. Around the camp, you'd see guys doing different jobs. For instance, you might see guys digging out a stump and then hauling it off in a wheelbarrow. Sometimes they'd make you dig a hole and fill it in again. For the most part, I did everyone's laundry more than I did lawn-type work. Sometimes we'd actually go into the little town of Willow River and sweep the streets with a push broom. They'd volunteer us for manpower to get that and other things done.

We did have some rec time where we could play basketball and stuff, and there was a gymnasium where we did our exercises. This is where we would play basketball. Sergeant Cook really considered himself a true basketball player, and one of the hardest things for me to do was not really be myself on the court. I found out early it was better to let him talk and act like he was the real thing than to play my hardest to beat him. Wow, that was tough for me! Sergeant Cook would choose up teams, always surrounding himself with guys who would complement his game.

Along with having a tight schedule, when we went from one activity to another, we jogged. I had played basketball all through prison and that helped me stay in shape, but I had gained some weight in prison because there isn't a lot to do but eat. Along with jogging everywhere we went, we also ran five miles every day. Of course, we didn't start out running the whole five miles right from the beginning. They worked us up to that. The facility had a track we could walk or run, but either way we had to do five miles. In fact, by the time you graduated, you had to run it. It was a good lesson in learning to work toward something, something that wasn't easy. I didn't really see it like that when I had to run it at the start. They built you up to it. By the time you got out, they wanted you to be able to run the whole five miles, and it really gave you a sense of accomplishment.

The only place we really had a chance to talk was in the barracks. The guy on the bunk below me was named Gerking. He was in his Bible every day and that was an influence on me. His Bible was obviously well used. It was marked up with lots of different highlights and also stuffed with papers from notes and whatever else was in there. When you see a guy reading his Bible in his spare time, it is very clear where he stands spiritually. You have to remember, we had very little spare time. It was precious, and he chose to give it to the Lord. Plus he went to church and was a man of integrity. He came from a wealthy family and his dad owned a bank. And even though he had the best of the few things we could have, like shoes, he was still in the same situation as me. I was really amazed at his ability to look at things in such a positive light all the time. God knew it was just what I needed!

It was no accident that God placed a Christian brother right under me. Plus, one other bunkmate was a Christian. We often talked about things of God when we were in our barracks. I started to go to church more often too. There were about twenty out of ninety guys who went to church. I started digging into the Word with a new spiritual hunger. I was doing a bunch of praying. I had always prayed through all my years in the darkness of addiction, asking God to get me out of it. Even when I was using, I'd pray. So many times I had felt hopeless. It was only the strength of God that kept me going. And now I was out of the darkness and drawing on God's strength in a new way.

Like I said, the barracks were the one place where we were able to talk freely, but even there, when talking to those in authority over us there was strict protocol to follow. For example, when we were getting ready to go out of the barracks, we were at liberty to ask things, like whether or not we could have our pants not bloused. But even in the barracks, we'd have to start the question with "Sir" and end with "Sir" or "Madam." You had to be very respectful, or you'd be doing a lot more pushups. To avoid the risk of asking something incorrectly and suffering the consequences, the guys would say, "Ask them this; ask them that." That way they could find out what they wanted to know without the risk of them suffering repercussions.

One thing that made me stand out from the other guys was the fact that I received letters from my friend, Deputy Commissioner of Correction Dennis Benson. Some of the guards saw the letters I received from Dennis and because of it, the people really didn't know how to handle me. I heard one of the drill sergeants say, "You guys know that Mark is buddies with the Deputy Commissioner?" But nothing came of it. A similar thing happened to me during my second time in prison when I was in Lino Lakes and Dennis had come for a visit. When he spotted me in the lunch hall he walked over to me and shook my hand. It could have put me in a bad spot, but it didn't. It was another seemingly small way that God's hand of protection was over me.

Here is "Choices and Changes" that I wrote during CIP. I include it here so you can see the work God was doing in my life:

First, I would like to introduce myself and tell you a little bit about who I am.

My name is Mark Foss. I am a forty-seven-year-old divorced father of two boys. I am a recovering drug addict and an inmate at the Challenge Incarceration Program, or CIP, in Willow River. I was born the fourth child of five in Hancock, a small farming community in west-central Minnesota. I have two older sisters, one older brother, and one younger sister, none of who use drugs.

I consider my childhood to have been a good one, though average. My father was a good man who worked at the local post office until his retirement. My mother was a homemaker and worked part-time outside the home. My parents were well-liked and respected throughout the community.

Growing up in a small town, much of our spare time was spent playing baseball, basketball, and football. Our town also had a city team that competed in an amateur baseball league; they were called the Hancock Orphans. When I was in the seventh grade, I became one of the batboys for the Orphans, whom a few years later I also played for, as my father before me did. One of the rituals that was a trademark of the Orphans was that after each game they would sit around and drink beer. As batboys, my friend and I would often fetch beers for the players and occasionally for ourselves too. It was at this time that I realized that a couple of beers would make me feel good. I thought that alcohol was harmless and even cool. My friends and I began to steal booze from our parents or had someone older buy some for us. Steadily my drinking increased and I eventually began to experiment with other drugs too. Little did I know that my bad habits of using back then would later destroy my life.

I enjoyed high school. I was recognized by the area coaches as one of the best players in the conference in both baseball and basketball. I broke my school's scoring record in basketball by 120 points. My grades were above average, and I enjoyed the benefits of being popular. My senior classmates voted me as most likely to enjoy life, best all-around, most talkative, and class cut-up. A couple of colleges had shown interest in my sports talent, and I was in love with my high school sweetheart. I felt like I was on top of the world.

The following year, I married my high school sweetheart and decided that I would pursue a college degree and play basketball. It didn't take long for my addiction to drugs and alcohol to ruin my plans. I had only been in college a couple of weeks when I was arrested for driving while intoxicated. After missing a couple days of school to straighten things out, I again returned to school. I was attending classes and working out with the team, but my drinking and drugging was out of control. I was arrested a second time for the same charge. This time the court costs and the missing of more school proved to be too much for me to overcome, and I was forced to drop out of school.

I never did get my addictions under control. I went from job to job. I was now getting drunk and high every day. My wife pleaded with me for fifteen years to quit using and be the man I was capable of being.

I've spent time in jails, prisons, and treatment centers over the years, but I either couldn't or wouldn't live a life in recovery. My wife finally decided that she needed to take our two young boys and herself and seek a better life. As sick as I was, I believe that at the time I was actually relieved that I would no longer have to listen to anyone lecture me and make me take an honest look at myself.

The years went by and I continued to use and sell drugs. In 1988, I was arrested for the sale of cocaine, methamphetamine, and marijuana to a Bureau of Criminal Apprehension agent. For two years he had befriended me while buying drugs and arranging for my arrest. I was shocked. I was sentenced to twenty-eight months in prison and was sent to Stillwater to do my time.

Upon my release I resumed my same old lifestyle. Using and selling drugs was a way of life for me. It wasn't until almost ten years later that I was again arrested, this time for felony fleeing a police officer and possession of a controlled substance, methamphetamine. I was sentenced to twenty-one months in prison.

While I was serving my sentence in Lino Lakes prison, I was brought the tragic news that all inmates fear – my father had died. There I was, in prison, surrounded by convicts who care little about how you are doing. I couldn't even cry or show any type of weakness. I had to be tough. The worst part was yet to come. Can you imagine the guilt and shame I felt when I went to my father's funeral flanked by two prison guards? I was crushed as I looked into the eyes of family and friends as I shuffled through the crowd.

Only a few weeks after this, I was watching the news when the location of the farm of one of my friends was shown on the television. It turned out that drug enforcement agents had surrounded his house. He came out of the house and pointed a gun at them and was killed. A short time after this another friend of mine in St. Cloud was murdered when a drug deal went bad. Since then, I've had another two friends end their lives with a single gunshot when their drug-induced lives seemed too hopeless to deal with.

After serving my twenty-one-month sentence I was again a free man. But again, I had spent my time in prison making new friends who could help me buy and sell drugs when I got out. Only two and a half years later, I was again arrested for selling drugs and here I am.

By now the State of Minnesota was tired of me, and I was sentenced to almost eight years in prison. After serving six months in the Stillwater prison in the Atlantis Chemical Dependency Program, I was transferred to the Moose Lake prison to await my entrance into the Challenge Incarceration Program. I was only there a few weeks when I was forced to deal with another death in my family, my oldest sister. All the feelings and circumstances that I had dealt with after my father's death haunted me again. The reality of prison seems so cruel and unfair sometimes.

Let me tell you a little more about prison. In prison you will be told when to eat, what to eat, and how much to eat. You'll be told when to get up and when to go to bed. They will give you the only clothes you can wear, which are just like everyone else's. You can either be locked up for twenty-three hours a day or you can work for twenty-five cents an hour. The showers are dirty and crowded. You won't have any privacy to use the bathroom, and it always stinks.

If you like to fight, then prison is the place for you. People are always looking for someone to fight. All you need to do is bump into someone or look at someone. Or maybe someone doesn't like the way you look or act. They might not like whom you hang out with. Someone might want your money or your shoes. Maybe they think you snore too loudly. In prison, people will fight for almost any reason. People will pay others to have someone beaten up. When you feel bad and need someone to talk to, your family is not there to help you. Right now my two sons are growing up without their dad.

Do you know that a high percentage of convicts are chemically dependent? Our prisons are full of people who may never get out because they did something very bad while they were high or drunk. I know people like that. Another thing people don't think about when they are using drugs is that they can catch AIDS, hepatitis, or other diseases that can kill them.

I'm here today to tell you that this time in prison is different for me. Since April 18, 2002, I have not taken one pill, one drink, or one hit. Nothing. I made a decision to turn my life around while I was attending the Atlantis Chemical Dependency Program in Stillwater.

****

While I was researching some of my past letters and things from when I was in prison, I came across a letter I had written on August 16, 2002. I had been in prison only a couple of days shy of four months. I was blown away by my attitude as I read my letter, only four months into a ninety-four-month sentence. The following is that letter, exactly as it was written (I believe God was speaking directly to me as I wrote):

It's Friday, August 16, 2002. As I lay on my steel bunk in cell 202, I wonder how it is that a forty-five-year-old intelligent, talented father of two has put himself in the position to be in prison doing his third bit for drug offenses.

The night is dark. Brilliant flashes of light are dancing off the cell hall walls and are accompanied by loud claps of thunder. I rise up on my bunk to gaze out the window at the wind-whipped rain. Occasional sheets of rain blow up against the window to obscure my view, only to dissipate as quickly as they come. The light from the rapid-fire lightning stops abruptly to leave me with an eerie reality of darkness.

I wonder, now, why I am driven to see a correlation between the weather and my own troubled existence. As I sit in the darkness and watch and listen, I feel the inner tugging of a spiritual message. My first thoughts are a loud, powerful, destructive happening, but the inner voice says, "No, look deeper."

As I sit calmly in awe, the rumblings from the heavens whisper to my soul the importance of where I'm at and what I am doing, and that I need to look at this experi-ence in a positive view.

It's then that I notice that the dirt is being washed clean from the handball court and travels in small streams to the drainage pipes below. I realize the grass is swaying happily in the wind as it sucks up nutrients and minerals essential for its life. I understand that all I see is only possible by the floodlights in the sky.

Still sitting on my bunk, I wonder how it is that an intelligent, talented father, who's seen many, many rains and storms, is visited with a fruitful message delivered to his heart. It's telling me that many of life's storms are really opportunities that provide the nutrients for spiritual growth. They give meaning and beauty to the quiet and calm as well as to the loud and thunderous. It helps me understand that a small tree that has never been tested by the breezes and winds could never survive a storm. The very wind that threatens its existence is really what makes it strong.

As I fix my gaze again on the cell hall windows, I am enveloped by a calm serenity. The flashes, rumblings, and rains have all ceased. I smile. I realize that it was not a storm at all, but a marvelous rain, a marvelous message, a message well received!

Mark Foss

(I'm waking up)

CHAPTER 11

Staying Connected

*If that is how God clothes the grass of the field,
which is here today and tomorrow is thrown
into the fire, will he not much more clothe
you—you of little faith?* (Matthew 6:30)

Looking back at times, I think of how the Lord began to work on me and change me from the inside out as soon as I surrendered my life to Him in the back of that cop car. I have thought about how the Holy Spirit works and have wondered if I started bearing the fruits of the Spirit right away or was it a slow process? This letter tells me that the Spirit was at work in me right away. The Mark Foss who was partying up to the day I went to prison could not have written that letter. Period!

While the Spirit began to change me immediately, His Word tells me that He also continues to work in and through me to this day. (*Being confident of this, that he who began a good work in you will carry it on to completion until the day of Christ Jesus.* – Philippians 1:6)

From there I was transferred to the Moose Lake prison where I continued to attend AA and to not use. After working hard for eighteen months to stay out of trouble, I finally entered the Challenge Incarceration Program or CIP. It was not easy. We worked hard on our minds and our bodies. We learned to adhere to strict schedules and follow many rules. We learned discipline and to change our way of thinking. We learned to be honest with ourselves and others. I would leave CIP with two and a half years of clean and sober time and a new chance at life. A life changed from the inside out. I needed to continue to attend AA and NA (Narcotics Anonymous) and surround myself with positive peers. I planned to work to reach goals and dreams again.

One of those goals was to help others like me recognize the dangers that drugs and alcohol present. I am one of the lucky ones. I still had family and friends who loved and supported me. I've had the opportunity and privilege to attend Atlantis and CIP, which together have helped me understand what it is I need to do to live a free and fulfilling life. I am not only thankful for this, but I run a ministry that brings this positive experience to others.

The choices each of us makes today determine whether we live a good and satisfying life, or one of pain and destruction. I hope all will choose life, freedom, happiness, and success. Leave drugs, alcohol, and a life of crime alone.

The Challenge Incarceration Program at Willow River was the first place my sons came to visit me. I felt more comfortable with letting them see me in that setting because there was no barbwire, no razor wire, and no walls. I had always been ashamed and didn't want them to see me in prison. But Willow River didn't look like a prison. Even how we dressed didn't make it look like we were in a prison. Instead of everyone wearing the same government-issue blue jeans and either a white t-shirt or blue button shirt, in boot camp we were all in uniform. My boys were about twelve and thirteen at the time they came to see me. We met in the place where we normally held church. They had set up some tables in there, and it was a more relaxed place to visit with loved ones. It wasn't stringent like prison visits.

I'm sure my appearance seemed very odd to them. I actually

looked like that guy in *Silence of the Lambs* (Hannibal Lecter). My head was shaved and I looked tough, as my hepatitis C was taking a toll on me.

My boys had really begun to get tall and Derrick seemed to have gained some weight. They looked good. I had talked to them via letters, but it was the first time I'd seen my boys in two and a half years. I'm sure Lorrie was uncomfortable with the idea of them coming to see me, but I was getting healthy again. I was allowed to hug them initially. They seemed bashful and kind of nervous, especially at first. With my head shaved and being a lot heavier since they last saw me, I'm sure it seemed strange to them, but oh, it was so awesome to see them. I recognized that God had really blessed Lorrie and me with them.

It was nice to see Lorrie again, too, even though our marriage was over. I felt embarrassed to sit in front of the woman I had once loved so much and hurt so much. Her reaction told me it would take a long time to get anyone to believe I had really changed.

Like I said, while I hadn't seen my sons, I did write to them. I wrote to others too. Writing letters was one way to stay connected to the outside world. I'd get letters every once in a while. Some of them were from Christians who encouraged me. Dave Schonberg and his wife, Jean, whom I mentioned earlier, stayed in touch with me. I had met him through his ministry when I was first in jail. He was always encouraging. It was as if he could see something in me I couldn't see myself. He ran a program similar to the one I run today. He had a little farm out next to the house he lived in and had four or five guys living there. After I was released, I also lived in a house he owned and worked the rent off. Eventually he sold me the house contract for deed when I got out.

His son-in-law, Jason, had a drywall job waiting for me so I could go to work as soon as I got out. The day after I got out of boot camp I had a job to go to. That's one of the things that stirred the idea that I had to do the same thing for other people.

Once I finished boot camp, I was on ICS (Intensive Community Supervision). When I finally got on the outside, my freedom had its limitations. I still had to call in, and I started out wearing an ankle bracelet to monitor my moves. Fortunately, it was removed fairly quickly. When I called in, I had to leave my daily schedule with them. They could show up at any time to give me a random drug test. I could be at my job site, in bed during the middle of the night – anywhere, any time. It didn't matter.

One day my ISR (Intensive Supervised Release) agent, Brian R., tracked me down when I was at a Goodyear tire dealer getting tires put on my van. I had my two sons with me, and when he showed up it upset me. I had to go into a public restroom and give him a urine sample in front of my sons. It really irritated me. When you get clean and know you're on the right path, you expect other people to believe you, but since you've been lying all your life, they don't. I learned my lesson not to get smart with him, though. He threatened to send me back, and he could. If you fail anywhere along the line, in any of the phases, they can send you back. I needed to keep my cool and treat him with respect. I thank God he didn't send me back. That would have been a bad memory to leave my sons with, to say the least. Today I work with Brian to help others.

Making it through CIP is not easy. I'd say about two-thirds of the people make it out of there and the other third are sent back. It's really a discipline. Before I went in there, I wasn't very disciplined and I was used to lashing out. I did what I felt, when I felt like it. The Lord used CIP to help me prepare for my new life on the outside. I got out of there on August 28, 2004, and I was blessed by the Christian man I mentioned earlier. Dave Schonberg put his faith in me. He helped me find a construction job and had a house waiting for me. He helped me get started with my new life on the outside.

I didn't take that help for granted. In fact, I realized how important that start was, and I felt led by the Lord to establish a ministry that would provide similar support for others in similar situations.

On August 28, 2004, I was released from CIP. Once again, I was confronted with the reality that lay before me of life on the outside. I had faced such opportunities for a fresh start many times before, including about ten treatment programs, many stays in county jail, and the two previous times in prison. Each time presented a chance for a new beginning. This was the third time, and the fresh start this time, for me, was different. Instead of leaving prison with an address book to go to other drug dealers and thugs, I left with my Bible and a new hope.

CHAPTER 12

New Life Inside and Out

Therefore, if anyone is in Christ, the new creation has come. The old has gone, the new is here! (2 Corinthians 5:17)

I believed if I ever had a chance for making something of my life, this was it, and in my mind, I figured it was probably my last chance. This time I wasn't just released; I graduated – in more ways than one. Graduation day at boot camp was special. After six grueling months of physical and emotional discipline, I was free again. That day all of the squad, including the sergeants, treated us really well. They congratulated us like we were people … people they were genuinely proud of. However, once the ceremony was over, my fellow graduates scattered. Many were met by wives or girlfriends, moms or dads, or a friend. We shared good-byes and split company.

I left CIP and moved to Alexandria. This time was different. My goal was to make it, to do it right. I focused intently on making the right choices this time around. It was time to start my new life, but while my life had changed from the inside out, much of my routine remained the same. I was to go directly to my residence and contact my agent.

I went straight to a house owned by Dave Schonberg. Dave was a large, gentle man. He stood about six foot three, maybe 240 pounds, with huge hands. He was known in the area not only for his love for Christ, but also for being called the "corn man" by many people, because he grew the best vegetables in the whole area. He owned some old REO Speedwagon trucks with a big flatbed on them and filled them up with corn. He'd load his pickup trucks and keep the trucks stocked, but he didn't sell on Sundays.

Dave had a jail ministry for many years. He was always there to greet people and lend a compassionate ear. And he always offered a message of hope. That's how I met him. He wouldn't leave me alone. When I was lost, his persistence was almost sickening. He was always gentle about it, but he wouldn't stop pestering me.

He ran a program at the Regeneration Center. The center had been started years earlier by a godly woman named Betty Coleman. Dave and his wife, Jean, had a farmhouse adjacent to their own home. They used it to take in men in situations like my own, men who had decided to get a new start on life and needed some help. The program really focused on being in a family setting, eating meals together, praying, and having devotions.

All of the Schonbergs were wonderful people with a heart for the lost and a devotion to Christ. I actually never entered into the program which Dave offered. Before I went to prison the last time, I did move into Dave and Jean's house with them for a short time, but I started using drugs again and I had to leave the house. As wonderful as the Shonbergs were to me, drugs were always my first priority. But even though that was the case at that time, I can't tell you how much the example of this family, of their love for God and life itself played a part in my eventual turnaround.

By the time I graduated from CIP, Dave Schonberg had bought another house. I had originally thought of going into Dave's program once I got out, but I told him I needed to be away from a men-only population. I had spent too much time living under those conditions. So while I originally planned on going into the Regeneration Program, I backed out because I was so sick of living with other men. Instead, I moved into the house Dave had recently purchased at 514 6th Avenue East. It was an old-style, two-story house with beautiful woodwork, three bedrooms, a dining room, and a spacious adjoining living room that opened up to a large screened porch. It was awesome, especially after living in a cell or even the barracks. Dave let me do improvements to pay toward some of the rent, and I later bought the house from him. He is a Christian who backs up what he believes with actions that matter.

Like I said earlier, Dave also had a job lined up for me. Along with that, he had arranged transportation for me. Because of my six prior DUIs, I hadn't had a driver's license for twenty years. But God used Dave to help overcome the various hurdles that could have given me a sense of hopelessness. I started work the next day even without a driver's license. I rode to work with Dave's son-in-law, Jason Koranda. He was a tall, handsome man with a stout spirit who understood my situation. Jason was known as one of the best drywall finishers in the city I lived in. He could do ten-thousand-square-foot houses by himself. His experience included work on many of the beautiful homes on the hundreds of lakes that surround Alexandria.

In my past, I had done my share of hanging sheetrock when I worked for a man by the name of Junior M. He was a man who enjoyed his socializing in the local pub, and I got to know him and became good friends with his sons, Jerry and Terry. A few years after I got out of CIP, God used Junior, his wife Kathy, and my friend Terry to help me secure my first loan to get LifeRight off the ground.

So on August 29 – the day after my release from prison – I had a job, a way to get to work, and a place to live. I was now keeping God at the top of my list. I did my daily devotions and brought EVERYTHING to Him in prayer. I wanted nothing to do with my old life, and I stood on the promises of God. John 10:10 says that *The thief comes only to steal and kill and destroy, but I have come that they may have life, and have it to the full.* God has been faithful!

I waited on the back porch for Jason to come and pick me up for my first day of work in society. Alexandria is a beautiful place to live with three hundred lakes within fifty miles. I gazed out at the alley beyond the small garage. I was filled with bridled optimism. I knew I had made changes, or I should say, God had made changes, but I was still concerned that my old desires for drugs and alcohol would come rushing back. But they didn't then and they haven't since. God truly gave me a new beginning – a fresh start from the inside out. I was a new creation.

CHAPTER 13

Living Amid Consequences of the Old Life

Whoever sows to please their flesh, from the flesh will reap destruction; whoever sows to please the Spirit, from the Spirit will reap eternal life. (Galatians 6:8)

Even though I had changed, there were still consequences that followed me from my past. When I first got out, I lived alone and under the strict supervision of an ISR agent. He had the authority to check on me any time, day or night. If I was going anywhere, I had to call ahead of time to tell him where I was going, what I was doing, and when I'd get back. His name was Brian R. Today, I work with him as we house some of the clients he oversees that are in the same position I was in back then.

My life seemed to be headed in the right direction, but loneliness crept in. Because I had always used drugs, alcohol, and the bar scene for my social life, I felt that my chance of finding a life partner was slim to none. But God!

It was a very cold blustery day in January 2006 when for some reason my truck pulled into the Caribou Coffee shop in Alexandria. I had never been in one before. Wondering how I ended up in a place where coffee had so many different flavors and cost so much, I walked in and noticed a beautiful young lady sitting cross-legged in front of the fireplace, reading her Bible. She didn't notice me. I wanted to talk to that woman, but couldn't find the courage to interrupt her study. I walked out and felt the Lord telling me to talk to her. I turned around, almost reached the door, then said "I can't do it." I retreated.

Noticing only one other car in the lot, I decided to put a card on her window stating that I was a Christian man and I didn't smoke, do drugs, or drink. I said if she wanted to talk she should call me.

My wife absolutely loves this story, and I have been threatened with bodily harm if I don't put it in here. I find it embarrassing, but true. After consulting with her mom, sister, aunt, and any other female she could think of, she eventually got around to calling me.

Being a recent graduate of MN. Teen Challenge, she was just what I needed for a friend. Nikol has been an inspiration to me and is feisty and willing to share her true feelings. Her beauty, great sense of humor, and love for Christ, make her the love of my life.

In all the years I worked in carpentry, I had avoided the finishing side of drywall work. I had always shunned the job of mudding with a passion, but working with Jason I not only learned it, I could do a good job at it. The one problem was that I was only making about ten dollars an hour. I started thinking about what I could do and came up with the idea of starting my own business. I worked for Jason for less than year when I decided to get my own contractor's license. By law, I had to wait six months before I could get my driver's license back, and after the six months that's exactly what I did. I got my driver's license back and Jason gave me a five-hundred-dollar van. Soon after, I started Mark Foss Construction. None of this would have been possible without the Lord putting the pieces in place.

When I started my construction business, I went back to Butch (Paul Erstad) at United Farmers and Merchant's State Bank in Morris and he gave me a chance. He could have easily said no to me because my credit was shot, but I was blessed with people giving me chances. I started my business and made regular payments, working to restore the credit I had damaged.

Later, I talked with Butch again and convinced him to let me buy a pickup so I could get my business off the ground. It was an old red Ford. I drove that for a while and then I asked if he would help me buy a work trailer. He did. Then I needed a bigger truck to pull it, and after about a year I had a business up and going. It took hard work, but it also took the grace of others to give me a chance to make it.

I'm not going to say mine was the best company in the world. I had felons working for me. I had to do a lot of babysitting, but I hired people like me whom no one else would hire. I wanted to help, but eventually I started a ministry that could reach out to these same guys. It became very apparent to me that God wanted me to take what I had learned and help others like myself, but it was going to take time for others to believe I was really a changed man.

I started to get visits from my sons who were now twelve and fourteen. They would be dropped off at my house or I would go pick them up with a friend. It was the first time in years that I had real time with them without someone listening in on our conversations or requiring that we keep our distance from each other. I had to get to know them all over again. I remember taking them fishing to Villard Lake where we could see the sunfish in the weeds. We caught many that day. I cherished that time and others with my sons more than I can put into words, but Lorrie still didn't trust me. She was very protective of the boys. It took a couple of years for her to trust me, and I couldn't blame her.

God began to really bless me. Small things in life meant something to me again. After decades of suppressing my feelings, I began to have emotions again, which was actually kind of scary. Only God could have opened the doors that were opened to me. I was out of prison and professing to be someone different. But why should anyone believe me?

I went to Jim R. in Morris and asked him to loan me some money to buy a house to fix up and sell. To my surprise, he said yes and loaned me $32,000. I stuck about $3,000 into the house and sold it for $60,000. But Satan had a plan to discourage me, even in this. As I waited to sell the house, I rented it out to a young couple with some small children. I even hired the man to work for me. A friend of mine who lived a short distance away called me one night when I was at a "Hood" meeting, and told me one of the children had fallen down the steep steps and was in really bad shape. I jumped in my car and drove down there. It was a very sad scene. I gathered around the family and prayed. The young boy died. I was devastated.

The next day I began to worry about my responsibility in all of this. Were there proper railings installed? I went to see Randy W. who was now sheriff. Randy was one of the officers responsible for sending me to prison the first time and since then had become sheriff. We had also struck up a friendship, and he told me not to be concerned about it. To make a long story short, what really happened was that the young man renting the house had hit the child so hard in a fit of rage that he almost tore his liver in half. The boy was the man's stepchild. As I went to all the court proceedings and the funeral, I wondered how the mom could still support this man. I can only pray he accepted the grace extended to him by Jesus.

Later Dennis B. and I bought a house together to flip. He financed it while I did the entire fixup. This was right when the housing market fell apart, so this one didn't turn out so good. I'm sure Dennis took a loss on this one, but he has never asked me to share in the loss. Dennis became a blessing and had the heart of a genuine friend who hoped that this time I would make it. In this life, he will probably never understand how much his influence and friendship helped me to make it.

Consequences came at me from my past in another way too. I remember attending church out at the Schonbergs' house on Sundays. One day, early in my relationship with Nikol, as we headed home from church I received a call. The call was from some very connected people who were offering me a chance to get back into the drug business in a big way. These were powerful people with a lot of money. Chills ran through my body, knowing who was on the other end of the call. I told the man no, that I was changing my life. As soon as I hung up, I deleted the number so my criminal thinking wouldn't win out and I'd call him back. I passed my first real test.

Life tested my newfound faith, but God is faithful. For a couple of years, Butch kept giving me chances with finances, and others did too. My small business was just that, but I was able to make a comfortable living each year. I never put ads in the paper to get the best guy for the job, but hired guys who needed a chance. I guess you could have called it a construction ministry. It also brought with it a lot of frustration, as guys wouldn't show up for work or sometimes did a poor job. More and more I realized, if I was going to do ministry, I needed to do it right. And it wouldn't be through my business.

My relationship with Nikol began to blossom. She saw my vision for a ministry and began to help me put it into action. Her having been through Teen Challenge was valuable in helping me lay the groundwork. She was a true inspiration with great insight on God, the Bible, and how the ministry should work.

In October of 2008, the Lord gave me a wonderful Christian woman to share life with. The Lord put two addicts, who had survived many very difficult and dangerous situations, together to move forward with the mission of helping others with the same challenges. We decided to start a ministry.

CHAPTER 14

LifeRight Campus

"For I know the plans I have for you,"
declares the LORD, "plans to prosper you
and not harm you, plans to give you hope
and a future." (Jeremiah 29:11)

I set out on a mission. I had a vision of what my (God's) ministry would look like and just began talking to people. I walked in to the Hilltop Lumber Company in Glenwood, Minnesota, one day and Dean Peterson was in there. I recognized him but he didn't recognize me. I looked really rough, as I was fighting hepatitis C along with the lingering effects of thirty years of heavy drinking and drug use.

I said, "Hi Dean." I could tell by the look on his face that he didn't recognize me. I told him who I was and that I was a Christian now. Dean eyed me with suspicion and wondered what I was up to now. A few months later, I called Dean up and asked him to meet with me. I had also run into Pat Conroy somewhere along the way and asked him to meet with me too. The three of us met at the Country Kitchen in Alexandria, sometime in early 2007. I presented my ministry idea and they liked it, but pointed out, "You don't have any money."

I said, "I'll get some."

Long story short, I returned to my old stomping grounds of Hancock and Morris and began talking to people about my vision. My first check came from Lloyd F. and my second from

Steve N. Those guys will never know how much they increased my faith in God that day as I headed back home with some significant seed money to show my first two original board members, Dean and Pat.

About that same time, I went to one of my friends from Hancock and asked if he would be willing to help me secure a loan to buy a church on three acres in Alexandria. With the blessing of his mother and father, Terry M. came through in a big way. God was moving!

The pieces for starting LifeRight started to fall into place. Against all odds, in December of 2007, LifeRight was granted its 501(c)(3) status, and in January of 2008, LifeRight opened its doors to minister to other men looking for a new beginning in the same way I had been. The facility started with a focus primarily on providing Christ-centered transitional housing to men coming out of jail, prison, treatment, or dealing with some other serious life issues.

However, starting the ministry was also a learning experience. It quickly became clear that these men needed more than a job and a place to live. If they were going to experience this "new life," they needed to get healing from the life issues that had landed them in this situation to begin with. When I first started this ministry, I would pick up a guy from prison and have a job lined up for him. Now I had a criminal with a job. It became apparent very quickly that the new life required an internal change of the heart that promoted internal governing to help them make better choices. If we did not take the time to instill godly values in them and get them to change how they think, we were wasting our time.

In April of 2009, through numerous "God incidences," I asked Jay Jenson to team up with me as the director of ministry. This ministry aspect of LifeRight took on a primary focus of helping these men understand there is healing through

Christ. While staying at LifeRight, the men are enrolled in a needs-based curriculum of Christ-centered courses. The aim of the program is to help them see who and whose they are in Christ – that they are precious, chosen, loved, and purposed men of God. With the leadership of Jay and his wife, Rochelle, who leads praise and worship, our church body, which is open to the public, has become a thriving and growing entity.

I could write a whole chapter on how God worked in the lives of Jay, me, and our wives for a time such as this. Why Jay's path never crossed with mine before this could only have been orchestrated by God. We ran in the same drug circles with the same friends – or more accurately – the same drug acquaintances. Jay was an ex-marine and I was a street fighter. I doubt we would have seen eye to eye if we had met before Christ came into our lives. We were baptized in a lake in Alexandria, just the two of us, by our pastor, John Taplin of New Life Christian Church.

I knew Jay's wife, Rochelle, from a group I had helped start called "The Hood." "Hood" stood for "Helping Others Overcome Deceit." It was a group of men and women seeking God with the prerequisite of having been in prison or jail. We were having a fundraiser at a local park to raise money to put a playground in a local trailer park that was a magnet for drugs and social problems. My wonderful girlfriend at the time, Nikol, and I went to this event. I saw Rochelle and we embraced each other with a casual hug, and she asked me who my friend was. I introduced them. "Nikol, Rochelle. Rochelle, Nikol." I barely got the words out of my mouth when the ladies let out screams as they realized that they were past friends from a very dark place in their lives who hadn't seen each other for about six years. Needless to say, both being clean and loving Jesus had changed them so much they didn't even recognize each other.

Jay lost his mother in 1999, and I lost my father the same year. We both had sisters with brain issues. We were engaged within a week of each other. We both had long marriages that failed, in my case 100 percent my fault. We both had three sisters and one brother. Jay's dad, "Jimmy Jenson the swinging Swede," and my mother are the same age.

Anyway, Jay has really helped grow this ministry. He heard the Lord telling him it was time to quit a job he had, and in a meeting one day, he did so on the spur of the moment. Not having any idea what he was going to do, I offered him the opportunity to start a Wednesday night service and he took me up on it. I even offered him a position as director of ministry. The only catch was that, like my own position, there was no pay. He accepted, and today his wife, Rochelle, takes care of most of the worship music while Jay delivers unbelievable messages of hope and grace.

Jay and I have implemented a kind of good-cop/bad-cop scenario in this ministry. I am not the most liked guy in the place, that is to be sure. I have come a long way, but I found myself being very impatient with guys who were there for the wrong reasons. The guys who have been around awhile tease me about one of my favorite lines: "Pack it up." As I continue to work with the men, I sometimes get quite loud and forceful, but I have learned to give correction in love and to always end on a positive note.

My thinking is that everyone who comes through our program is there voluntarily. I don't care if they want to continue to destroy their lives (yes, I really do); just don't do it at LifeRight. Be man enough to move out. It is especially hard to get gang members to quit their old lifestyle, as they have more hurdles than most to overcome.

I need to add that Jay, a self-taught minister of God's Word, is one of the most gifted and genuine Christian speakers you will ever hear. I encourage you to go to our website, LifeRightoutreach. org, and listen to his podcasts.

During this journey, God brought into our lives a steering committee of twelve men and women who love God. After meeting with these people, they conveyed their hope of having a LifeRight in the city of Willmar. After several months of planning, God moved in a big way. They ended up purchasing a property worth over a million dollars, for only $142,000. This enabled us to house up to forty men there and turn one of our houses here in Alexandria into a women's ministry. In July 2014, both facilities were opened. We were suddenly able to help a combined fifty men and ten women. Cecil Meyer and Chris Alle are local Willmar men who help run the facility. Al and Dave, good friends of mine and participants in our program, work as cooks and in maintenance. One of their primary goals is to be a Christ-like example to the men at LifeRight.

Our church body is amazing. We have members from all walks of life: some covered with tattoos and others who are businessmen and women. We have more men than women, the way God intended, as men are to be the spiritual leaders of the house. Our church has Christian graffiti on the walls painted by men who have gone through our program. Our seating consists of regular folding chairs with a mixture of couches, love seats, and cushy chairs. Slogans like "No perfect people allowed" or "Come as you are" that adorn our walls are an indication of what we are about. You see, at LifeRight Outreach, we will always point you to God.

What now? Where do I go from here?

By the grace of God I am what I am, and his grace to me was not without effect. (1 Corinthians 15:10)

Here we are, November 17, 2014. As I sit in my office and reflect on what God has done in my life over the past twelve years, I can't help but feel a deep sense of gratitude and love for my

Lord and Savior, Jesus Christ. The desire for drugs and alcohol is long gone. My feelings of failure and inadequacy have vanished, though I do at times feel the weight of my past. The planning, scheming, and manipulating to make deals to get drugs is over. I love my life.

Last week I went to court and I have now been awarded my gun rights back. I've shot my share of pheasants, as I again enjoy the hunt that I gave up many years ago when drugs took over my life. After not having a driver's license for about twenty years, I now drive a lot. I'm getting ready to go deer hunting tomorrow (legally) for the first time in decades. I will be hunting on property that some dear friends of mine, Gordy B. and his wife, Cindy, gifted to LifeRight. There's a small log cabin surrounded by thirty-four acres of hunting land and over eleven hundred feet of lakeshore. Gordy has been my personal, as well as LifeRight's insurance agent for the past ten years.

The desire of Gordy and Cindy to sacrifice that beautiful property to give us the opportunity to use it for the hurting, searching, broken, and lonely as a retreat is another example of God's grace. We have already baptized eleven people out there and celebrated with about one hundred and fifty by roasting some hog and praising the Lord.

Freedom, right? I will tell you right now that as marvelous as all that is, none of it would ever have been possible without my total surrender to Jesus on my way to prison on that gloomy day, April 18, 2002. That is where the real freedom comes from. Part of that freedom, for me, includes breaking free from the attitude that let Satan keep ahold of me by having thoughts of *Why try, I won't be able to do it anyway,* or thinking that if I got straight and became a Christian I wouldn't be able to have fun anymore. However, I will tell you that being a true follower of Christ is probably the hardest thing I've ever done but also the most rewarding.

My God is a God of restoration. I have been blessed with two wonderful sons, Derrick and Brendon. We have an awesome relationship. The pain and sorrow of a failed marriage – 100 percent my fault – has been replaced with a sense of respect as Lorrie and I strive to make our new marriages the best they can be. Both Lorrie's husband, Gary, and my wife, Nikol, have joined the family to add two more caring parents to the mix. I am a very proud father, as both my sons were valedictorians of their class, like their mother. We've all been able to follow the boys all over the state and north-central United States watching them play football, basketball, and baseball. Derrick and Brendon played for the University of Minnesota Morris, with Derrick as a quarterback and Brendon a receiver. Many times I have been blessed with the words, "Foss to Foss," over the loud speaker during both high school and college football games as Derrick threw the ball to his brother Brendon. It was an honor to drive Brendon to Indianapolis for an NFL combine. They are both hard workers and avid hunters.

I have a wonderful and beautiful wife to share my life with as we both strive to become the precious and chosen children of God we were created to be. Nikol's family is loved and treasured by both of us, as is her aunt Marlene and the late John Nelson and his family. My family has been restored and I'm able to do what I believe God has called me to do at LifeRight. Both my sisters Annette and Lori have great lives and we love each other dearly. They have good families and work hard being who God created them to be. My brother Brad and I are closer than we've ever been, and his family loves the Lord. Mom is happy, healthy, and doing great

Jay and I and our wives have dedicated our lives to helping men and women who suffer similar afflictions as we experienced in our pasts, and to overcome them and walk in victory. We are able to share firsthand the victory we have in Christ. We share

Why did I decide to write a book?

It's important that you know that without Christ in my heart, there is no good in me. I write this book to give hope to the hopeless. I want to start a fire in people's hearts and put a sparkle in their eyes. You see, if I can do it, anybody can do it! I'm pretty sure, if you would have lined up a hundred people who struggled with drugs and alcohol and said one of them would get clean and start a successful and growing Christian ministry, I would have been almost the last one anyone would have thought would do that.

I have had some tell me that I need to give myself more credit, but I can't. You see, I tried treatment at least ten times. I tried many times to quit drinking and using drugs, only to come up short. Then one day I surrendered my life to Christ and everything changed. That is now my clean date, April 18th, 2002, nearly thirteen years ago.

I would like to see copies of this book in every prison in the United States. As I travel from prison to prison and speak with these men and women, I find our thinking patterns are almost always the same. I know the loneliness and hopelessness of addictions. I've experienced the feelings of failure. I was a failure as a son, a spouse, a father, a friend, EVERYTHING! You see, if Satan can get our minds, he's got us. If people will understand who we are and whose we are (children of God), there is hope and victory. When I put my trust in God, He did more than I ever thought He would. By the way, God is always doing more than we think He is. (*Now to him who is able to do immeasurably more than all we ask or imagine, according to his power that is at work in us* – Ephesians 3:20.)

Since surrendering my life to Christ, my life has been

blessed over and over again by God. He has done this through the many friends He has placed in my life. I am overwhelmed when I see people whom I used to sell to and use drugs with from Morris, Willmar, Benson, Alexandria, and other towns come through our doors in search of a new life in Christ. People who recognized that their way hasn't worked and want a new chance at life. People who knew how hopeless I was and decide to give Christ a try.

Along with the victories come many heartaches, however. Last winter we had to bury a brother in Christ. He sadly chose to take his life in the wrong direction, but we know that as a believer in Christ, Chris will reside in heaven with our Savior. God will always sacrifice the body for a soul. Even yesterday a man who came through LifeRight, only to go back to his own ways, tried to commit suicide. Others leave and try to have one foot in the world and one foot walking with Christ. The world usually wins for a season. It's awesome to see these brothers and sisters in Christ swallow their pride and come back again. We call it "going around the mountain again." Jay and I are always and will always be here for them till we too are called home.

I know that there are those who wonder when I will fall. I will tell you right now that I won't. You see, I worked very hard to earn the reputation as a hellion, and now I'm working hard to prove "I'm not the man I used to be." I am far from perfect and work daily to become a better person in the eyes of my Lord. He knows my heart, and He created me. There is nothing I can do to make Him love me any more or any less. (*But God demonstrates his own love for us in this: While we were still sinners, Christ died for us.* – Romans 5:8) Our God is a God of grace. It is our belief that once you accept Jesus as both your Lord and Savior, your name is written in the Lamb's Book of Life, and Jesus promises to never blot it out (Revelation 3:5).

Does this mean we can go on sinning and be right with

God? I believe that once a person realizes the magnitude of what Christ did on the cross for them, they no longer will want to sin. Will I still slip sometimes? Yes, we were born sinners. But I will also strive to become a better person every day, for God's glory. My heart will be right in front of God because I love him and realize how much he has done for me. Someday this life will pass away, and all that's left is eternity with or without God.

I will NEVER use drugs or alcohol again. The Lord has delivered me from that. For me to use again would be like not recognizing what Jesus did on that cross for me or saying that He didn't do enough. It would be like slapping Him in the face. I refuse to let Satan win.

Where do I go from here?

LifeRight is my life. As I move forward in this ministry with my wife Nikol, Jay and his wife Rochelle, and the rest of our wonderful staff, I know we will continue to help change lives. We have had over two hundred and forty men and women come through our program to date. That number will increase very quickly, as our Willmar facility has the potential for forty to fifty residents. We currently have about forty men in the program and seven women.

Our ministry has become much more than a housing program. We are known all over the state as a place where men and women without hope can come and get loved on. We have never turned anyone down because of funding. For this reason, we are in a constant battle to make ends meet, but God provides. With the leadership of Jay, our Wednesday and Sunday night services are growing rapidly (Tuesday night in Willmar). We have our services at 6:30 in the evening so as to not compete with the other churches in town. Our church family consists of people from all walks of life. Two of our favorite sayings as a church are "No perfect people allowed" and "Come as you are."

So, life goes on. No longer do I stress over the things of my past, but rather I continue to grow in Christ. I no longer worry about how others perceive me, because my LORD is my judge as well as my ROCK. He made me just the way He wanted me to be, to do a job specifically for me, to help the broken, lonely, searching, and hurting people He puts in my path. This year was the first year since I opened LifeRight that I visited my home town of Hancock in a setting where I could invite the entire community. I find it hardest to go back there, as I'm fully aware of the skeptics and naysayers. Do I blame them? NO. Even Jesus said in Matthew 13:57: *"A prophet is not without honor except in his own town and in his own home."* Not that I'm a prophet. I'm just a man who loves God and wants to serve him and share my powerful testimony with others..

My days are filled with the circumstances of people's lives. Some are good, many are bad. One thing I know for sure is that since that day, in the back of that squad car, God showed up in a big way. I believe that God has been pursuing me my whole life. It just so happens that the only way He could get my attention was when all that was left was Him and me. My total surrender was critical. Am I still a sinner? Of course. But I'm working on that.

There will be those who discount what I have to say and that's fine. I will always point you to God, not to man. To have experienced the miracle of total freedom from drugs and alcohol cannot be overlooked. In my own power I tried to quit many times.

Here are a few verses that describe where I am at:

Not that I have already obtained all this, or have already arrived at my goal, but I press on to take hold of that for which Christ Jesus took hold of me. Brothers and sisters, I do not consider myself yet to have taken hold of it. But one thing I do: Forgetting what is behind and straining toward what is ahead, I press on toward the goal to win the prize for which God has called me heavenward in Christ Jesus. (Philippians 3:12-14)

You see, apart from Christ I am nothing. I owe everything to Him. *But as for me and my household, we will serve the LORD* (Joshua 24:15).

Do you have a personal relationship with Jesus Christ? The Bible is either ALL LIES or ALL TRUTH. John 3:3 says: *"Very truly I tell you, no one can see the kingdom of God unless they are born again."*

I am hoping believers and non-believers alike will turn to Christ and really seek a relationship with Jesus. It's more than knowing about Him. It's knowing Him.

I praise God the minute He allows me to open my eyes in the morning. As I get my coffee and eagerly dive into the Word each morning to start my day, I experience the blessing of knowing *his compassions never fail. They are new every morning* (Lamentations 3:22-23). You no longer will hear me cuss and never will you hear me take the Lord's name in vain. As a man who helped destroy lives for years, I hunger and thirst for the opportunity to be a vessel for God, to bring people into His kingdom too, and, as the Bible instructs, to *always be prepared to give an answer to everyone who asks you to give the reason for the hope that you have* (1 Peter 3:15).

So I will continue down the path God has orchestrated for me. The concerns of the past have changed. They have gone from darkness to light, from hopeless to hopeful, from defeat to victory. Each day brings fresh revelation of the challenges that lie ahead, but now I have the assurance that *no weapon forged against you will prevail* (Isaiah 54:17).

Satan will use whatever has worked before to get you to believe you are not worthy to be a child of God. Whether it is guilt, shame, abandonment, fear, etc., he will try to take your hope away. Stay strong; the victory has already been won.

The snow is falling, the temperature is dropping, and the winds are blowing, but calm and warmth are in my heart. I'm thinking about maybe going and finding some snow to plow through, some mischief to kick up. You see, I'm still a rebel, but I'm a rebel for Christ!

I've got it! I know a family on a long, winding, snowy road that could use a Thanksgiving Day turkey. "Come on Trooper!" (my German Shepherd pup). "Let's go for a ride, and God, would you please drive? You know the roads much better than I do."

About the Author

Mark Foss grew up in a small farming community in west-central Minnesota. His childhood was good, free of worry and pain. He became an accomplished athlete, especially in basketball. Then it all changed. He became his own worst enemy and lived the next thirty years as a drug dealer and an addict. The gifted and talented teen was gone, and a hard, destructive man took his place. This life carried him to the edge of death, despair, and even insanity . . . until he met the Lord Jesus Christ.

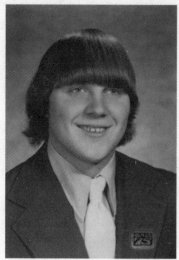

Mark Foss – graduation photo

Mark's mug shot

Mark at New Direction boot camp, 2004 – Third from left, back row

Mark and his wife Nikol

Mark – with sons Derrick and Brendon

LifeRight Outreach men - brothers in Christ

LifeRight Outreach – outdoor grounds

Mark and Jay – with LifeRight Outreach truck

Mark and his wife Nikol, and Jay with his wife Rochelle

jubilee
B I B L E 2000

*Hear what God is
saying through this
original translation*

ANEKO Press